Horrible Geography

RAGING RIVERS

AND

ODIOUS OCEANS

Two Horrible Books in One

ANITA GANERI
MIKE PHILLIPS

SCHOLASTIC

Scholastic Children's Books,
Commonwealth House, 1–19 New Oxford Street,
London WC1A 1NU, UK

A division of Scholastic Ltd
London ~ New York ~ Toronto ~ Sydney ~ Auckland
Mexico City ~ New Delhi ~ Hong Kong

Published in this edition by Scholastic Ltd, 2005
Cover illustration copyright © Mike Phillips, 2001

Raging Rivers
First published in the UK by Scholastic Ltd, 2000
Text copyright © Anita Ganeri, 2000
Illustrations copyright © Mike Phillips, 2000

Odious Oceans
First published in the UK by Scholastic Ltd, 1999
Text copyright © Anita Ganeri, 1999
Illustrations copyright © Mike Phillips, 1999

ISBN 0 439 96083 5

Printed and bound by Nørhaven Paperback A/S, Denmark

10 9 8 7 6 5 4 3 2 1

The right of Anita Ganeri and Mike Phillips to be identified as the author and illustrator of this
work respectively has been asserted by them in accordance with the Copyright, Designs and
Patents Act, 1988.

Contents

Raging Rivers

Introduction	7
Wild West by river	11
Going with the flow	16
Running away to sea	37
Scraping the bottom	59
Wet'n'wildlife	77
Raging river living	94
Raging river roving	114
River rage	134
Revolting rivers	154

Odious Oceans

Introduction	163
Going down…	166
The odious oceans	170
Plenty more fish in the sea	199
Oil and other ocean spoils	220
Ocean locomotion	239
Odious exploration	260
Deep, dark and … dangerous	281
Sea sick	304

RACING RIVERS

INTRODUCTION

Geography is full of horrible surprises. Take learning about rotten rivers, for a start. One minute, you're sitting in your nice, warm classroom, nodding happily off to sleep while your geography teacher's voice goes on and on and on...

TODAY'S LESSON IS ALL ABOUT FLUVIAL BEDLOADS.* OPEN YOUR BOOKS AT PAGE BLAH, BLAH, BLAH...

* That's the tricky technical term for a river's sandy bottom.

You close your eyes and start to dream... You're sitting on a grassy riverbank, a long, cold drink in one hand, a fishing rod in the other. Lovely. The sun is shining, the birds are singing, geography doesn't seem so boring after all. Bliss.

Suddenly, your dream turns nasty. Really nasty. Now you're standing in the pouring rain, up to your knees in muddy water. Feeling like a drowned rat. What a nightmare. Yes, your teacher's taken you on a ghastly geography field trip. And it's HORRIBLE.

So horrible that you're glad to wake up and find yourself back in your geography lesson again. It may be boring but at least it's dry.

But not all geography is dismally damp and uncomfortable. Some bits are horribly exciting and interesting. Try this simple experiment. Smile sweetly at your mum, dad or guardian and tell them you're off for a bath. Don't wait for a reply, they'll be too shocked to speak. Go into the bathroom and turn the taps on full. How long does it take the bath to fill up? About ten minutes? Now try to imagine 200 MILLION bath taps turned on full. This is how much water it takes to fill the awesome Amazon, the biggest river on Earth. (Back in your bathroom, pull out the plug, flap your towel around, and pretend you've had a good, long soak. Your grown-up will be ever so impressed.)

And that's what this book is all about. Long enough to stretch right around the world, strong enough to carve out mile-deep valleys, angry enough to flood a whole town, with wicked waterfalls as tall as the Eiffel Tower, rushing rivers are all the rage. In *Raging Rivers*, you can...

- explore the world's greatest rivers with Travis, your intrepid tour guide.

- take the plunge over the world's highest waterfalls.

- catch and cook a piranha for lunch (mind your fingers).

9

• learn how to survive in a flood (against all the odds).

This is geography like never before. And it certainly isn't boring. All you have to do is keep turning the pages. You don't even need to get wet. Unless, of course, you drop your book in the bath…

The amazing adventures of Lewis and Clark
Washington DC, USA, 1803

The two young men summoned to President Thomas Jefferson's office shivered slightly, although the room was warm. They had just been handed the most important mission of their lives – to lead the first ever official expedition across the wild west of America to find a river route to the Pacific Ocean.

Jefferson's idea was to open up these lands for trade and settlement, and to make America richer and more powerful than ever before. There was just one problem. No one had explored these vast lands before. No one knew what dangers lay ahead for them or if they would ever make it back home. It was enough to make anyone shiver. President Jefferson shook their hands and wished them goodbye and good luck. He didn't care what other people said. He was sure that he'd found the right men for the job.

The two men in question were dashing Captain Meriwether Lewis, the President's trusty private secretary, and Lewis's old friend, Lieutenant William Clark. They were young, strong, brave and handsome. They'd need to be all of these things (OK, so good looks weren't that important). It was going to be a long and rocky road. Lewis and Clark put their heads together and soon they'd hatched a daring plan. They would travel up the Missouri River, as far as they could go, cross the Rocky Mountains, then follow the Columbia River to the Pacific. Simple!

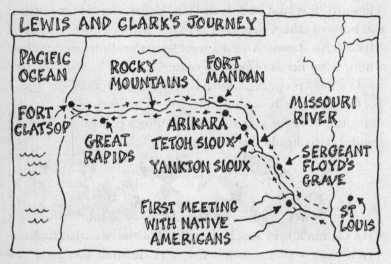

LEWIS AND CLARK'S JOURNEY

PACIFIC OCEAN

ROCKY MOUNTAINS

FORT MANDAN

MISSOURI RIVER

FORT CLATSOP

GREAT RAPIDS

ARIKARA
TETOH SIOUX
YANKTON SIOUX

SERGEANT FLOYD'S GRAVE

FIRST MEETING WITH NATIVE AMERICANS

ST LOUIS

They spent the winter preparing for the expedition. They were not travelling alone. With them went a group of 43 men, mostly soldiers, grandly named the Corps of Discovery. They also took six tonnes of food (when this ran out, they'd have to hunt for more), weapons, medicines, scientific equipment and gifts for the local people.

These were loaded into three sturdy boats – one barge and two canoes. These were crucial. Without good boats, it was sink or swim.

At last, on Monday 14 May, 1804, everything was ready. A single shot was fired to signal the off and the expedition headed out of the town of St Louis on the banks of the Missouri. It would be two and a half years before they would see home again. From St Louis, they followed the mighty Missouri as it wound westward, through rolling green plains where huge herds of buffalo roamed. For five months, they made steady progress. Canoeing upriver, watching the world go by, was really quite pleasant. The only flies in the ointment were the swarms of mosquitoes constantly buzzing around their heads. Very irritating.

In October, they reached the land of the Mandan Indians. They were warmly welcomed, and decided to spend the winter there because the river would soon be covered in ice.

The winter of 1804–1805 was very long, very cold and very boring. On some days, temperatures plummeted to a teeth-chattering low of -40°C. The members of the expedition stayed snug and warm (but bored stiff) inside their log cabins. It was far, far too cold to risk setting foot outside those four walls.

By the following April, they were all glad to be on the move again. There was just one tiny hitch. So far, they'd been able to follow their route on some roughly-drawn charts but from here on the maps ran out. Completely. What lay ahead was utterly unknown territory. Without maps, Lewis and Clark had no idea what they were in for – whether or not they'd be hiking up mountains, wading through rivers or hacking their way through vegetation. There was just no knowing. And they could only hope that they were going in the right direction!

But plucky Lewis and Clark weren't worried. They hired a local Indian guide to help them out – someone who did know the lay of the land – and continued upriver to the Rocky Mountains. Now came the worst part of the journey. Crossing the mountains was a terrible ordeal. Their food ran short and at night the weather turned bitterly cold. All the men could do was grit their chattering teeth and keep plodding grimly on.

Their courage paid off. On the other side of the mountains lay wide open plains … and the Columbia River. Finally, on 7 November 1805, they sailed down the river to its mouth in the sea. At last, they had reached the Pacific Ocean and their journey's end.

The following spring, they began their long journey home again, reaching St Louis on 23 September 1806. Lewis and Clark were given a hero's welcome. Everyone was glad to see them, especially as they'd been given up for dead. They'd covered some 7,000 kilometres, most of it by canoe. They'd been growled at by grizzly bears, rattled at by rattlesnakes, and riddled with frostbite, fear and starvation. Lewis had even been shot in the leg by someone who mistook him for a deer! It's true! Despite this, only one man in the team had died, probably from appendicitis. The expedition had been a raging triumph. True, their river route was not very practical. If you weren't a brave explorer, it was much too long and dangerous. (Many Americans did later follow in Lewis and Clark's footsteps, in search of new lands and trade, but they sensibly went overland by wagon.) Geographically, though, it was all a rip-roaring success. Lewis and Clark's expedition journals were crammed full of maps, sketches and notes about the rivers they'd sailed down and the people they'd met. (They kept notes about absolutely everything. That's the sort of thing geographers do.) Places and people that horrible geographers had never seen before.

GOING WITH THE FLOW

Of course, good old Lewis and Clark weren't the first people to realize just how horribly handy rivers can be. They used rivers to get them from A to B. But people have also been drinking them, washing in them, fishing in them and generally messing about in them for years and years.

The Romans even built a city on one. According to legend, the city of Rome was built by two brothers called Romulus and Remus. They were identical twins. Their mum was the priestess Rhea Silvia. Their dad was Mars, the god of war. So far, so good. The one bad apple in their happy family was their wicked great-uncle, cranky King Amulius.

* That's Roman for cheese.

Great-uncle Amulius was worried sick that one day when the twins were older they'd try to seize his throne. So he shoved them in a basket and chucked them into the raging River Tiber. As well as saving his royal skin, it would save him a fortune in birthday presents.

The twins drifted downstream and came to a stop at the bottom of the Palatine Hill. There a she-wolf found them. But instead of wolfing them down for lunch, she took them home and brought them up to be nice, well-behaved, er, wolves.

Later, they moved in with a kindly shepherd. (They had to promise not to chase the sheep.) But they never forgot their happy wolfhoods and decided to build their old wolf-mum a splendid city on the spot where she'd found them. For her retirement.

Building began. But things soon went horribly wrong. Romulus and Remus fell out big-time, over the height of a wall! You see, Romulus built the wall to defend the city from attack. But Remus said it was useless, way too low to stop anyone. And to prove his point, he jumped over it.

Romulus was furious. Did the twins make up? Nope, they did not. Romulus pulled out his sword and killed Remus. Then he named the riverbank city after himself.

So, if you believe your legends, Rome was built next to the River Tiber by a pair of twins brought up by a kindly wolf. Sounds reasonable.

Teacher teaser

Outwit your teacher with this Roman river talk:

What has Jenkins done?

What on Earth is a raging river?

Some bits of geography are horribly difficult to understand. Don't worry, you can leave those bits out. This book is about the other bits, the bits that will turn you into a genius geographer without any effort at all. Take raging rivers, for instance. Your teacher may try to bamboozle you with all sorts of boring and baffling facts about rivers. Take no notice. It's just your teacher trying to make himself or herself feel important. Pathetic, eh! The horrible truth is that a river is a stream of freshwater (that means it's not salty like the sea) that flows across the land. Simple

Water on the brain

You might think that yummy chocolate milkshake is the most useful and precious liquid on Earth. But you'd be wrong – dead wrong. While you could go for weeks without a milkshake, without water to drink, you'd be dead as a dinosaur in a few days. And where does most of this water come from? From raging rivers, of course. Rivers might only make up one per cent of the Earth's water, but that one per cent is fresh water which, when it's been cleaned, we can drink.

ARE YOU SURE THIS WATER'S BEEN CLEANED?

The first person to study water seriously (well, it takes all sorts) was British scientist, Henry Cavendish (1731–1810). Henry was born in Nice, France but spent most of his life in

London. Now nice Henry was a bit of a loner. He lived with his dad, until his dad died, and didn't go out very much. Well, you wouldn't either if you'd had Henry's dire dress sense. His favourite outfit was a hopelessly unfashionable purple suit, with a frilly collar and matching cuffs, topped off by a threadbare three-cornered hat. It looked frightful. No wonder Henry didn't have many friends. He certainly didn't have a girlfriend. In fact, he wouldn't even allow girls to set foot in his house. He thought they were a bad influence.

Luckily, Henry had one saving grace. He was absolutely brilliant at chemistry. He spent most of his time in his house, doing chaotic chemistry experiments. (He much preferred chemistry to people. After all, test tubes couldn't talk back.)

Anyway, when lucky Henry was 40 years old, he inherited a million pounds. He was rich! But did he let the money go to his head? Oh no. Did he blow all his cash on fine wine, fancy clothes or exotic holidays? Nope, he did not. He continued to work as hard as ever and spent most of his lovely lolly on … guess what? You've got it, it went on yet more chemistry kits and chemistry books. And it was just as well for horrible geography that it did because not long afterwards Henry Cavendish made the most amazing discovery. One day, in his laboratory, he mixed up some hydrogen and oxygen gas in a jar and heated the mixture up. What do you think he saw?

a) The sides of the Jar covered with soot?

b) The sides of the Jar covered with water?

c) The sides of the Jar covered with slime?

Answer: b) The sides of the jar were covered with water. What brainy Henry had discovered was that water is not made of one single substance (i.e. plain old water) as single-minded scientists thought. In fact, it's made up of two gases, hydrogen and oxygen. The reaction between the two created water vapour which condensed (turned into liquid water) when it touched the sides of the jar. Incredible. In chemists' code, freshwater is called H_2O. That means two hydrogen atoms and one oxygen atom joined together as a water molecule. And billions and billions of wonderful water molecules make up a raging river.

Today, someone like Henry might be called a horrible hydrologer. That's the posh name for a geographer who studies river water. And hooray Henry was frightfully posh. Both his grandfathers were frightfully posh dukes who left Henry pots of frightfully posh dosh!

Earth-shattering fact
But where on Earth does all this horrible H_2O come from? It can't all be made in chemistry jars. And how does it get into raging rivers? Here's an Earth-shattering fact for you to flow with. The water found in raging rivers has flowed millions and millions of times before. In the water cycle, it's recycled again and again. So the water flowing in the awesome Amazon may once have flowed through Ancient Rome. Mindboggling, eh? To see how the water cycle works, imagine you're one of hard-working Henry's marvellous molecules. (Better still, imagine your geography teacher as one.) OK, so you'll have to use your imagination!

You're about to go on a very long journey. Over the page there's a picture to show you the way. Are you ready to go with the flow?

4 THEN MILLIONS OF DROPLETS GANG TOGETHER TO MAKE A CLOUD. THE SEA LOOKS A LONG WAY AWAY NOW.

5 INSIDE THE CLOUD THINGS ARE REALLY MOVING! OTHER MOLECULES ARE BASHING INTO YOU AND JOINING YOUR DROPLET UNTIL IT'S TOO HEAVY TO HANG AROUND. LOOK OUT! YOU'RE GOING FOR A LONG JOURNEY BACK TO EARTH. YEP, YOU'RE FALLING AS RAIN...

6 YOU MIGHT FALL INTO A RIVER WHICH CARRIES YOU TO THE SEA. YOU MIGHT FALL ON TO THE RIVER PLAIN AND TRICKLE INTO THE RIVER. YOU MIGHT SOAK STRAIGHT INTO THE GROUND. (OR YOU MIGHT FALL STRAIGHT INTO THE SEA.) BUT YOUR JOURNEY'S NOT OVER YET. NO WAY! IT'S ABOUT TO START ALL OVER AGAIN!

How on Earth do rivers flow?

1 Rivers always flow downhill. Which seems horribly obvious when you realize that they're dragged down by gravity. It's the same when you go downhill on your bike. You don't need to pedal – gravity does all the work. Gravity is a force which brings things down to Earth. It's what keeps your feet on the ground. It happens when a large object (the Earth) pulls a small object (the river or you on your bike) towards it.

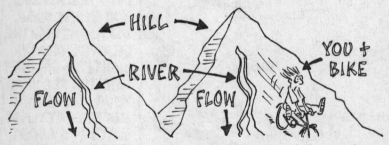

2 A river doesn't always flow at the same speed. It speeds up and slows down. This isn't because the river gets tired, it's because of a force called friction. You get friction when two objects try to push past each other and slow each other down, like when you're out shopping and get stuck in the

crowds. What's this got to do with rivers? Well, sometimes, friction between the river (Object No. 1) and its bed and banks (Object No. 2) slows the water down. A river flows fastest on the surface, near the middle, where friction is much weaker.

See how fast a river flows

What you need:

- a stopwatch
- a tape measure
- two sticks
- an orange
- a river

What you do:

a) Measure out a 10-metre stretch of river bank. Mark the start and end with the sticks.

b) Drop the orange into the water.

c) Time the orange as it flows downstream. (That's the direction the water's flowing in.)

d) Now for some boring maths. (You can skip this bit if it's too much like homework.) Remember how some bits of river flow faster than others? To work out an average speed for the whole river, you need to multiply your answer by 0.8. For example, if the orange travels 10 metres in 20 seconds, the flow speed is 0.5 metres per second. If you times this by 0.8, you get an average of 0.4 metres per second. (Experts use average speeds to work out things like how much water the river carries. But that's for another maths lesson!)

3 Rivers flow fastest down steep slopes, and you don't get much steeper than a waterfall. The Niagara River speeds up to 108 km/h as it plummets over Niagara Falls. That's about 16 times normal walking pace. Time to get your running shoes on!

WOW! A RUSHING, RAGING RIVER!

4 At any time, there's only enough water in all the world's rivers to keep them flowing for about two weeks. Without fresh supplies, they'd quickly dry up.

5 The Ancient Greeks had some funny ideas about what gets a river flowing. They knew all about the water cycle and all about rain. (A right bunch of know-alls they were.) But they didn't believe for a single minute that enough rain could fall to fill even one raging river.

They thought that the water must come from the sea, flowing into rivers through underground streams (and somehow losing its salty taste on the way).

6 In 1674, French lawyer, politician and part-time hydrologist Pierre Perrault measured the amount of rain falling in a year over the land drained by the River Seine.

What did he find? He worked out that there was enough rain to fill the Seine six times over and still have some left over for a quick wash. The clever-clogs Greeks had got it wrong!

7 Horrible geographers now know that water gets into rivers in four different ways. And they all start with rain. Here's Travis to guide you through them.

Some rain falls straight into the river. Simple!

Some rain falls on the ground. It runs downhill into small streams which flow together to make a river.

Some rain falls to the ground and freezes into glaciers. When the weather warms up, parts of the glaciers start to melt. This starts a stream, you can guess the rest!

ICE

Some rain falls and soaks into the ground. Boringly, it's called groundwater. Some of it flows straight into rivers. And as the rivers flow downstream, some rainwater gushes up as a spring.

UNDER GROUND

8 Luckily, rivers don't have to rely on groundwater for the whole of their water supply. Just as well. They'd be waiting a very long time. Groundwater flows very slowly. Very slowly indeed. This is what one scientist said about it:

Another scientist, American John Mann, decided to see if this snaily tale was true. You can try his slimy experiment for yourself.

What you need:

- a tape measure
- a stopwatch
- a snail
- plenty of spare time on your hands

What you do:
a) Take the snail out into your garden.
b) Put it down on the path.
c) Time how long it takes the snail to trail along for a metre. (If you get bored waiting, cut the distance down.)

What do you think happens:

a) The snail leads you up the garden path?

b) The snail moves at a snail's pace, obviously?

c) The snail moves faster than go–slow groundwater?

Answer: c) From his experiment, John Mann worked out that groundwater moves at only $\frac{1}{70}$th of a snail's pace. That's 70 times slower than a slowcoach snail! And who said doing science experiments wasn't boring!

Raging river record breakers: test your teacher

After all this flowing to and fro, you'll need a well-earned rest. Why not veg out on the sofa, put your feet up and leave the hard work to somebody else? Somebody like your geography teacher! Test their hydrological know-how with this quick quiz.

1 The Nile is the longest river on Earth. TRUE/FALSE?

2 The Amazon holds the most water. TRUE/FALSE?

3 The shortest river is D River. TRUE/FALSE?

4 The Rhine is the longest river in Europe. TRUE/FALSE?

5 Some rivers are usually dry. TRUE/FALSE?

6 Some rivers are completely frozen in winter. TRUE/FALSE?

Answers:

1 TRUE. The record-breaking Nile in Egypt is 6,695 kilometres long, making it officially the world's longest river. But it's a very close thing. The Amazon in South America is just 255 kilometres behind. Some horrible geographers see things differently. According to their measurements, the Amazon comes out longer. (Note: don't worry about these differences. Geographers are always falling out. You see, geography isn't an exact science, which means nobody knows anything for certain. So although geographers like to think they have an answer for everything, it isn't always the same answer!)

2 TRUE. The awesome Amazon carries more water than any other river on Earth, 60 times more than the Nile and one fifth of all river water on Earth. At its mouth, the Amazon empties 95,000 litres of water into the sea. EVERY SINGLE MINUTE! That's like emptying out 53 Olympic-sized swimming pools. Compared to this raging river, the Nile's a mere trickle.

3 TRUE AND FALSE. It's true that, at just 37 metres long, D River in Oregon, USA, is the world's shortest river. It flows from Devil's Lake into the Pacific Ocean.

4 FALSE. The vulgar Volga in Russia is 3,530 kilometres long and the longest river in Europe. The Rhine is only 1,320 kilometres long, less than half the Volga's length.

5 TRUE. Many desert rivers hardly ever have any water in them. Because there's so little rain in the desert, they're dry for much of the year. Other rivers are wet in winter and dry in summer.

6 TRUE. Every winter, the Ob-Irtysh River in snow-bound Siberia freezes along its whole length. The upper part of the river, high up in the mountains, stays frozen solid for five whole months. Brrr!

What your teacher's score means...

Allow two points for each correct answer. And no cheating...

10–12 points. Excellent. With such in-depth knowledge, your teacher will make a top hydrologist.

6-8 points. Not bad but the answers aren't quite flowing yet. If your teacher paid a bit more attention in class, he/she might just stay on course.

4 points and below. Oh dear! I'm sorry to say but your teacher's far too wet for this type of work. Better stick to teaching...

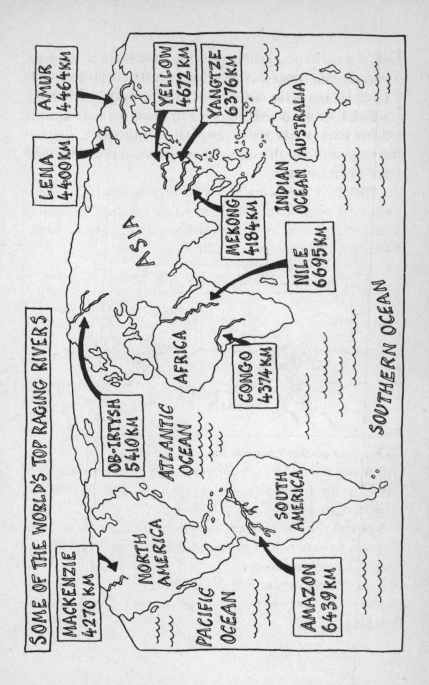

SOME OF THE WORLD'S TOP RAGING RIVERS

MACKENZIE 4270 KM

OB-IRTYSH 5410 KM

LENA 4400 KM

AMUR 4464 KM

YELLOW 4672 KM

YANGTZE 6376 KM

MEKONG 4184 KM

NILE 6695 KM

CONGO 4374 KM

AMAZON 6439 KM

NORTH AMERICA

SOUTH AMERICA

ASIA

AFRICA

AUSTRALIA

PACIFIC OCEAN

ATLANTIC OCEAN

INDIAN OCEAN

SOUTHERN OCEAN

Had a good rest? Feeling ready for anything? I hope so. You're going to need all your energy for the thrills and spills waiting for you in the next chapter. You're about to follow the course of a raging river all the way from its start until it reaches the sea. Are you ready to go with the flow? Time to put on your life jacket – just in case your canoe capsizes and you end up falling in!

Rivers are a bit like people. They change as they get older. When they're young and just starting out in life, they rush about energetically and are full of get up and, er, flow. As they get older and more mature, they slow down and take things easier, meandering gently through middle age. Finally, old age catches up with them. As they near the sea and their journey's end, many get slow and sleepy, and a bit grumpy if you wake them up suddenly. Sound like anyone you know?

The river: a turbulent life story

Stage 1: Young river. At this youthful stage, the raging river's really flowing fast. It's a river in a hurry. And it's bursting with youth and energy. It's so strong it can carry horribly heavy rocks which scrape out the shape of its bed and banks.

Stage 2: Middle age. The river's starting to slow down now. It can't see the point of all that rushing about. It's dropped the rocks – they're much too heavy – but it still lugs along loads of mud and sand. And instead of smashing straight through obstacles, it sensibly meanders around them. Very grown up.

Stage 3: Old age. Now the river's so sluggish and slow it starts to drop off … zzzzzz, sorry, it starts to drop off all the mud and sand. Now and again it overflows its banks and floods but then it has to have a good, long rest until finally it flows into the sea.

Stage 1: Young river

Source: OK, folks, good morning and welcome on board. My name's Travis and I'm your tour guide for today. And I don't mind telling you, you're in for a real treat. If you've got any questions, be sure to ask. As long as they're not too difficult!

So here we are at the source of the river – the place where our raging river begins and the start of our turbulent tour. The source might start off as rain falling on a mountain top or springing up from underground. (Water springs up out of the ground like this when the ground isn't "spongy" enough to absorb it.) Is everybody ready and comfy? It's all downhill from now on!

Drainage basin: Hello again. Wakey, wakey! If you look to your left and right, you'll see the river's drainage basin. Sorry, what was that question? Yes, the lad at the back. Oh, I see. No, it's not the thing your mum uses to drain veg or pasta for your tea! It's the land which supplies a river with water. Some rivers have horribly huge drainage basins. The Amazon's covers about 6.5 million square kilometres. That's twice as big as the whole of India. Gi-normous, I think you'll agree!

Tributary: See that little stream flowing in from the right? No, the right, sir, that's the left. Does anyone know what it's called? No? Oh well, never mind.

Geographers call it a tributary. No, madam, I don't know why they can't just say stream either. Believe me, it would make my life easier. But some tributaries are raging rivers in their own right. Take the Amazon again. It's got more than a thousand tributaries. One, the Parana, is among the longest rivers in the world.

Waterfall: And now for the most exciting part of our tour. I love this bit! Is everyone feeling brave? Plucky enough to take the plunge? I'm sorry, madam, it's much too late to turn back now. Even if you're feeling seasick... Hold on tight. You're about to have a jaw-dropping ride over a waterfall. A waterfall's where the river plummets over a step of hard rock (see page 66). Close your eyes if you're scared of heights. Here we goooooooo...

Stage 2: Middle age

Trunk: Wow! What a splash! We'll just stop here for a minute while I count up and make sure you're all here. Never mind, madam, it can happen to anyone. Now we're on the main bit of the river. Which has nothing to do with elephant's noses or trees. Though you could say that tributaries look a bit like branches growing from a tree trunk. If you were trying to be clever. Or poetic. The trunk is the bit that gives the river its name, like Nile, or Amazon, or, er, D. Get the idea? What's that, sir, you don't understand? I'll be along in a minute to explain.

Valley: See those high-rise slopes on either side? That means we're in a V-shaped river valley. It's been carved out of the rocks by the forceful flow of all that water (see page 59).

You get a splendid view from the top. But you'll need to take another tour for that, we've still got a long way to go. Don't worry, madam, we'll sort you a ticket out later. Put your purse away before it gets wet.

UP STREAM ←

DOWN STREAM →

Meander: Now I know that it seems we're going around in semicircles but rest assured, it's the river, not you, that's going round the bend! These great snaky S-shaped loops you can see in the river are called meanders.

Yes, sir? Good question – why are they called meanders? They're named after the meandering River Menderes in Turkey. No madam, we don't go there on this tour. To meander off course just for a moment, here's a quick diagram to explain how they work:

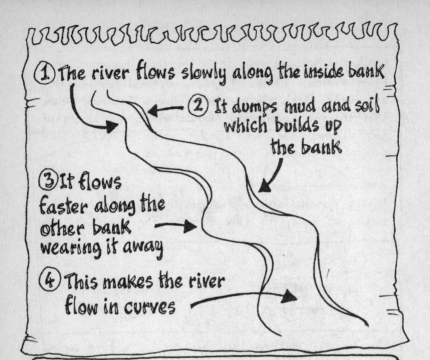

① The river flows slowly along the inside bank

② It dumps mud and soil which builds up the bank

③ It flows faster along the other bank wearing it away

④ This makes the river flow in curves

Ox-bow lake: Look at that lovely banana-shaped lake away to your left? No, not a banana-shaped cake, miss. We'll be having lunch in a very short time. That's right, madam, over there. It's called an ox-bow lake and it's where the river's cut straight across a loopy meander. Anyone want to take a photo? I would if I were you. It'll be no good leaving it till later - the lake may well have dried up by then.

Stage 3: Old age

Floodplain: See all that thick, gooey mud on your left and right? That's the river's floodplain. The mud means that the river's gone and flooded and tipped tonnes of goo all over the land (though other floodplains are covered in sand). It might not look very much, madam, but the mud's packed full of minerals which make brilliant plant food. Fruit and veg just love it. Which is why floodplains make fantastically fertile farms. And talking of food, it's time to stop for lunch!

Mouth: And here we are, folks! The mouth of the river and journey's end! Sadly, this is where we leave our river behind and watch it flow out into the sea. Here it drops the rest of its load of mud and sand. Some of this builds up into a delta (see page 73). Some of it's washed out to sea. And that's where you get off, folks! It's been great meeting you all, and I hope you've enjoyed the trip. Please be careful when leaving the boat. It might take a few moments to get your land legs back. And if you'd like to leave a small-ish tip, I've left a hat at the back. Thank you and see you soon!

Earth-shattering fact

Meanders may look bone idle, meandering along without a care in the world. But mind out if a meander's on the move near you. For years, the town of New Harmony in Indiana, USA, stood firmly on the banks of the Wabash River. The river meandered away meekly to the west. True, one loop was heading towards the town but at a snail's pace. There was nothing to worry about. Surely? Then one day in 1984 it started to flow faster, FOUR TIMES FASTER. At this rate, the town would soon be sunk as the river ate away at its foundations. Plans have been made to reroute the river and cut the earth-moving meander off. Will it work? The people of New Harmony are still waiting to see.

WHERE'S MY RUBBER RING?

Teacher teaser

Next time a teacher asks you what you want to be when you grow up (boring!), pretend to think hard for a moment, then say:

OH, I'M PLANNING TO BECOME A FAMOUS LIMNOLOGIST

Is that some sort of doctor who treats arms and legs?

The source of the problem

If your river tour hasn't left you soaked to the skin, think back to the place where it all started. Its source. There are three different types of sauce, sorry, source. No, not tomato sauce, cheese sauce and parsley sauce, or anything else you find lumps of in your school dinner. The *source* of a river is usually high up in mountains.

Can you match these three famous rivers to their sources? Go on – it could be the start of something really big.

Raging rivers to choose from:
1 River Ganges
2 River Amazon
3 River Rhine
Suitable sources to choose from:
a) a leaky lake
b) a glassy glacier
c) a springing mountain stream

Answers:

1 b) The source of the Ganges is a glacier in the Himalayas. They're very high mountains in Asia. In spring and summer, the tip of the glacier melts and starts off a stream which grows into the River Ganges. The Ganges flows right across India to the Bay of Bengal in the east. For many people, it's a holy river which fell from heaven and they worship it as a goddess. Below the glacier is a village called Gangotri. Thousands of pilgrims brave the wintery weather to travel here each year to worship the goddess and bathe in the icy river water. Brrr!

2 a) The awesome Amazon starts off as a trickle from a tiny lake high in the Andes mountains in Peru. The trickle flows into a stream called the Apurimac. That's the local word for "great speaker" because of the noise it makes as it roars downhill. From the lake, the Amazon flows right across South America (a staggering distance of 6,440 kilometres) to the Atlantic Ocean. Here it pours so much water into the sea that the sea doesn't start to get salty for another 300 kilometres.

3 a) and c) The raging Rhine begins life as two mountain streams flowing from the Swiss Alps. One glugs from the end of an icy glacier. The other leaks from a lake. The two join forces but they're not alone for long. Lots of other streams muscle in on their act. Then the river flows across Germany and Holland into the North Sea.

The sorry saga of the search for the Nile's source

You might think that finding the source of a river would be quite simple and straightforward. Surely even a horrible geographer couldn't miss a mountain stream? Especially if the river in question is incredibly long and famous, like the raging River Nile. Easy peasy, you might say. No problem. But you'd be wrong. Horribly wrong.

For hundreds of years, horrible geographers searched high and low for the source of the Nile. They knew that it must be somewhere in Africa, but Africa was a horribly huge country and most of it hadn't yet been explored. Several intrepid expeditions had set off to search for the source (including one sent by the nutty Roman emperor Nero). All of them returned in failure. Where on Earth did the Nile begin? It remained one of geography's best-kept secrets. Until one day in 1856, when two daring British explorers set off for Africa to really get to the source of the problem, once and for all. Their names were Richard Francis Burton (1821–1890) and John Hanning Speke (1827–1864).

Part I: The search begins

On 19 December 1856, Burton and Speke landed on the island of Zanzibar in the Indian Ocean. From here, they planned to head into Africa where the search would begin. They planned to venture into parts of Africa where no Europeans had ever set foot before.

But they didn't have time to worry. Stocking up for the journey took most of their time. They needed enough supplies to last the whole trip – they reckoned on it taking at least a year – and some porters to carry everything. (They were going to be much too busy exploring to carry anything themselves!) Among all the boxes and boxes of scientific instruments, books, tools and medicines, the two men allowed themselves some small luxuries, including a box of cigars, four sturdy umbrellas and a dozen bottles of brandy. For medicinal purposes, of course.

By June 1857, everything was ready and they finally set sail for Africa. Their route took them inland, then west to Lake Tanganyika. Then they would head north to the mountains to search for the secretive source. For eight hard months, they travelled on.

The heat was horrible, the flies were terrible, and the local people weren't always friendly. But Burton and Speke knew they could put up with almost anything if only they could find the source. Anything, that is, except each other.

The problem was that Burton and Speke were about as alike as chalk and cheese. As happy in each other's company as sausages and lumpy custard. You see, Burton was already a famous explorer, with several expeditions to Africa under his belt. He was brave and brilliant at everything, including speaking 29 languages. But he was also bolshy and looked rather odd. This is how an acquaintance described him:

HE HAD A COUNTENANCE THE MOST SINISTER I HAVE EVER SEEN, DARK CRUEL EYES LIKE A WILD BEAST. HE HAD THE BROW OF A GOD AND THE JAW OF THE DEVIL.

Speke, on the other hand, was boringly neat, tidy and respectable, everything beastly Burton was not. He was also horribly stubborn. He might not be as brainy as Burton, but wasn't about to be bossed about. No way. Burton and Speke just about managed to stick together until they reached Lake Tanganyika but by then they were barely on speaking terms. Fortunately for them both, they were too ill to argue. Burton could hardly move his legs and had such murderous mouth ulcers he could not eat. An illness had left Speke almost blind and he'd gone deaf because of a beetle buried in his ear.

HMM! I WONDER WHAT'S IN EAR?

But what about the source of the Nile, you ask? Had they forgotten why they were there? Who better to spill the beans than Burton? Here's how he might have described the rest of the journey in his secret diary (He did keep a real diary of the expedition but it probably didn't go quite like this.)

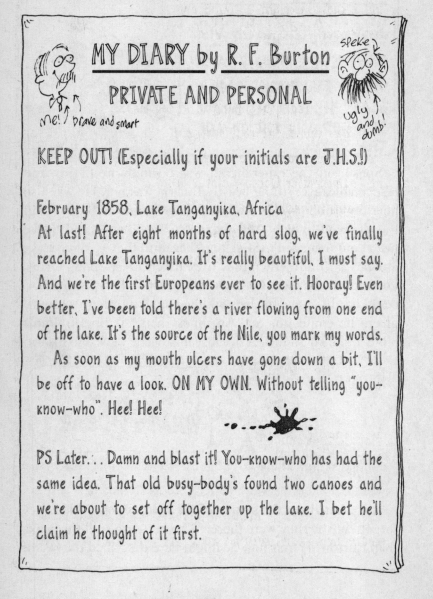

MY DIARY by R. F. Burton

me! brave and smart

speke

ugly and dumb!

PRIVATE AND PERSONAL

KEEP OUT! (Especially if your initials are J.H.S.!)

February 1858, Lake Tanganyika, Africa

At last! After eight months of hard slog, we've finally reached Lake Tanganyika. It's really beautiful, I must say. And we're the first Europeans ever to see it. Hooray! Even better, I've been told there's a river flowing from one end of the lake. It's the source of the Nile, you mark my words.

As soon as my mouth ulcers have gone down a bit, I'll be off to have a look. ON MY OWN. Without telling "you-know-who". Hee! Hee!

PS Later... Damn and blast it! You-know-who has had the same idea. That old busy-body's found two canoes and we're about to set off together up the lake. I bet he'll claim he thought of it first.

PPS Still later. . . We didn't find it. I'm a bit disappointed but I know I'm right. I always am.

September 1858, Kazeh, Africa

You'll never guess what's happened now! That dreadful sneak Speke's been at it again. Trying to make out he's so clever. He's really beginning to annoy me. He only claims that he's found the real source of the Nile. . . ALL BY HIMSELF! According to him, he's found another lake that he's named after Queen Victoria (What a creep! What does he want, a medal?) and he says that it's definitely the source of the Nile. Of course, it isn't. What a fool! I told you he was being ridiculous. He's just jealous that I beat him to it. When I asked him to prove it was really the source, he got rather twitchy so it's obviously all just a guess. Anyway, I'm sick of it. No one's to mention the "N" word again. As far as I'm concerned, the subject is CLOSED.

May 1859, London, England

This time he's really gone too far. He really has. When we went our separate ways, he PROMISED to wait until I got home to tell people about his stupid theory. I might have known he couldn't keep his word. Grrrr! He's not only gone and told everyone, but they've sent him on another expedition to see if he is right! Well, he's really pulled the wool over their eyes. It makes me so MAD! Don't worry, let him think he's won for now. But I'll be back, and when I am ... I'LL SHOW HIM!!!

September 1864, Bath, England
Speke's gone and done it again! It really is unbelievable! Five years I've waited to get my own back. Five long years. And, guess what, he's only gone and got himself killed! Some people are so selfish. And it wasn't even in Africa. He'd come home, spouting some drivel about the question of the Nile's source being settled, and getting on everyone's nerves. He still hadn't got any proof, you see. (What did I tell you?) So it was decided that he and I would have the whole thing out face to face, man to man, once and for all. We'd fixed the meeting for 16 September when news came that he'd been shot in a hunting accident. The idiot! The lengths some people will go to! (Actually, I'm secretly quite upset but don't ever tell anyone I said so.)

Part II: The search continues

DAVID LIVINGSTONE...

A JOLLY NICE CHAP

It now fell to Britain's most famous living explorer to take up the search for the source. David Livingstone (1813–1873). Even his name filled people with confidence. Livingstone was ideal for the job. For a start he was terribly nice and got on well with everyone. (Eat your heart out, Burton.)

So, in August 1856, he set sail from England for Africa. Livingstone thought that both Burton and Speke were barking up the wrong tree. He thought that the true source of the Nile was a river to the south. But the expedition to find it was a disaster. Before very long, half of his companions had died, deserted or fallen ill. Livingstone himself was very ill and lost touch with the outside world.

WHEN'S THE NEXT BUS HOME?

HE'S BARKING MAD!

Years went by. Back in Britain, poor old Livingstone had now become Britain's most famous given-up-for-dead explorer. Luckily, people in America hadn't quite given up on him and a journalist from the *New York Herald* newspaper was sent to

Africa to find him. (Oh, and to settle the question of the source of the Nile – but you've heard all that before.) His name was Henry Morton Stanley (1841–1904).

To cut a long story short, on 10 November 1871, Stanley finally found Livingstone.

After meeting Livingstone, Stanley was well and truly bitten by the exploration bug. After a short trip to England for fresh supplies, he returned to Africa to check out the claims made by Burton, Speke and Livingstone. And three years later, after many trials, tribulations and horrible hardships, he finally did everyone a favour and solved the mystery of the source of the Nile, once and for all (this time he really did).

So, where on Earth was it? Which one of our three intrepid explorers had been right all along? Was it:

a) Bad-tempered Burton and Lake Tanganyika?
b) Sneaky Speke and Lake Victoria?
c) Long-lost Livingstone and the River Lualba?

Answer: b) Speke turned out to have been right all along. (Burton was furious!) The source of the Nile was a river which flowed from Lake Victoria over a waterfall called Ripon Falls. It was bad luck for Burton – he believed that the river flowed from Lake Tanganyika instead. But the river in question flows into the lake, not out of it. And Livingstone might have been good with people but he got his rivers wrong. His River Lualba flows to the south of Lake Victoria. But Stanley later proved that it flows into the colossal River Congo and nowhere near the Nile.

Raging river fact file

NAME: River Nile
LOCATION: North Africa
LENGTH: 6,695 km
SOURCE: Lake Victoria
DRAINS: 3,349,000 sq km
MOUTH: Flows into the Mediterranean Sea on the coast of Egypt.
FLOW FACTS:
● The longest river on Earth.
● Its two main branches are called the White and Blue Nile because of the colour of their water.
● The Ancient Egyptians lived along its banks.
● What they said about it: "He who once drinks the water of the Nile will return to drink again." (Ancient Egyptian proverb)

MEDITERRANEAN SEA
EGYPT
SUEZ CANAL
NORTH AFRICA
SUDAN
NILE
WHITE NILE
LAKE VICTORIA
BLUE NILE

So, the source of the Nile was found at last. And the riddle of the river was solved. But the story of rivers doesn't stop there. Oh no. The source is only the beginning. Your raging river adventure's got a long way to run. So, dash downstream and into the next chapter...

You may think that rivers aren't good for much except meandering along to the sea. But you're way off course. Even the laziest rivers are hard workers. Running water is horribly powerful. So powerful that, over millions of years, it can change the face of the landscape for ever. (Your teacher's stoniest stare may wipe the smile off your face but even it can't rattle solid rock.) But water doesn't work alone. The river drags along tonnes of rocks, mud and sand which give it its cutting edge. But how on Earth do they do it? Here's a step-by-step guide to earth-moving erosion*.

*That's the tricky technical term for the way rivers run over the ground and gradually grind it down. It can all get horribly wearing!

How on Earth does erosion work?

1 Horrible geographers always want their own way, like having their own word for everything. But they can't simply call a river a river. That would be far too easy. Take all the rocks and mud a river carries. They can't just call it rocks and mud, they have to call it a load. Boring, or what? The load can be anything from boulders the size of double-decker buses to miniscule grains of sand.

2 Some of the load dissolves in the water. These are the bits that make water hard and leave scaley bits in your kettle. Some bits float along with the water. The biggest rocks and

pebbles sink to the riverbed and roll or bounce along the bottom. Boring geographers call these the bedload.

RAGING RIVER

DUCK!

DISSOLVED BITS
(OK, SO YOU'LL HAVE TO IMAGINE THESE)

LARGE ROCKS BOUNCE ALONG

FLOATING BITS

LARGE ROCKS ROLL ALONG

BEDLOAD

RIVERBED

3 Pure water is almost clear and colourless. But who wants a boring river like that? Most rivers are muddy brown. But not all of them. The Yellow River in China is, you've guessed it, yellow! (It's also called the Huang He.) That's because of the tonnes of yellow soil which blow off the land and into the water. Making it so horribly muddy that the Chinese say that if you fall in, you'll never get clean again. (Why not try this next time you need an excuse for not washing?) They also say, "When the river runs clear," for something that's never likely to happen.

4 Some of the load scrapes and rubs away at the river's bed and sides, like a giant piece of sandpaper or a scouring pad. (That's a spongy thing for doing the washing up. Ever heard of it?) Other bits bash the rocks up like a huge hammer. No wonder the rocks crumble under the pressure.

5 The faster a river flows, the bigger and heavier the rocks it can carry and the quicker it grinds the ground down. As the river slows down in middle age, its load grows but is mostly made up of light mud and sand. Near the sea, the river runs out of energy and dumps its load. It can't erode any more land away. It's too much like hard work.

GO AND WASH YOURSELF OFF IN THE RIVER!

BUT THAT'S HOW I GOT INTO THIS MESS!

6 Erosion's often so slow you can't see it happening. To notice the difference, you'd need to stick around for millions of years. This is how long it takes to carve out ghastly gashes in the ground called valleys. They're shaped like the letter "V". (You sometimes get valleys with no river because the river's dried up and left the valley behind.) Gorges are valleys with very steep, sheer sides. Not the places to visit if you suffer from vertigo. (That means you daren't look down.) But if you've got a good head for heights, why not check out our brilliant competition? (Don't set your heart on winning, though.)

THE GREAT

★ GRAND ★

CANYON

COMPETITION

Your chance to win the trip of a lifetime to gawp at the Grand Canyon in Arizona, USA where you can really soak up the atmosphere! A holiday you won't forget in a hurry...

AND GUESS WHO'LL BE YOUR GORGE-OUS TOUR GUIDE?

Prize includes:
* Return tickets for two to Arizona
* A signed copy of Travis's *My Grand Canyon Guidebook*, packed with hints and tips about what to see and do
* A free photo of you with your favourite mule

MARVEL AS YOU MAKE YOUR WAY DOWN ON MULEBACK!

DARE TO LOOK OVER THE EDGE!

GASP AS YOU GLIMPSE THE WORLD'S DEEPEST GORGE!

TREMBLE AS YOU RIDE THE RAGING RIVER RAPIDS!

TO ENTER, ALL YOU NEED TO DO IS ANSWER THE THREE QUESTIONS OVER THE PAGE – IF YOU DON'T KNOW THE ANSWERS, JUST GUESS. THEN MARK THE GRAND CANYON ON THE MAP. HERE'S A CLUE – YOU'VE ALREADY READ THE ANSWERS!

HORRIBLE HOLIDAYS – THEY'RE ALL THE RAGE!

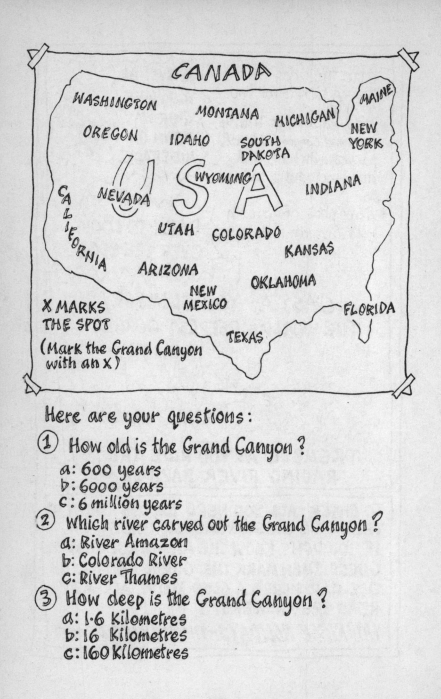

CANADA

WASHINGTON

OREGON

IDAHO

MONTANA

MICHIGAN

MAINE

NEW YORK

SOUTH DAKOTA

USA

WYOMING

NEVADA

CALIFORNIA

UTAH

COLORADO

INDIANA

KANSAS

ARIZONA

OKLAHOMA

NEW MEXICO

TEXAS

FLORIDA

X MARKS THE SPOT

(Mark the Grand Canyon with an X)

Here are your questions:

① How old is the Grand Canyon?

a: 600 years
b: 6000 years
c: 6 million years

② Which river carved out the Grand Canyon?

a: River Amazon
b: Colorado River
c: River Thames

③ How deep is the Grand Canyon?

a: 1·6 Kilometres
b: 16 Kilometres
c: 160 Kilometres

Answers: – NO PEEKING IF YOU'RE ENTERING THE COMPETITION!

1 c) But the rocks on either side of the Canyon are much, much older than that. Near the top they contain fossils of plants and animals which lived about 250 million years ago. Near the bottom, the rocks date back about 2,000 million years. Ancient or what!

2 b) The Colorado River rages along for over 2,000 kilometres from the Rocky Mountains in the USA. It used to flow into the Gulf of California in Mexico but so much water's been taken out of the river for farming and drinking that it no longer reaches the sea. For about 446 kilometres, it flows through the lowest part of the Grand Canyon.

3 a) The Grand Canyon is an awesome 1.6 kilometres deep. That's like looking down from the top of a 444-storey building! Ooooh! And it's a pretty sheer drop from the top to the bottom. If you dare make the descent, you can ride down on muleback or hike down on foot. Either way the trip takes several days and you'll need to watch your step – you wouldn't want to disturb a deadly rattlesnake. If you're too tired to climb back up again, why not take a boat downriver. Mind the Big Drops, though: they're the rapids ahead.

Rapids are a stretch of very fast-flowing water. You'll find out how to ride them, and how to survive them, when we get to page 110. You're safe for now!

D'YOU EVER GET THAT SINKING FEELING, SIR?

Going over the top

But it's not just valleys that feel the full force of raging rivers. Imagine you're a young river. (Go on – you can do it!) You're racing along in full flow when a band of hard rock blocks your way. What do you do? You could either a) keep right on flowing or b) give up and go home? You'll keep going? Good, giving up and going home's for wimps. But get ready for a bumpy ride. If there's softer rock lurking below, you could be about to take the plunge. Here's the inside story of how a waterfall's formed:

1 The river flows over hard rock, with soft rock underneath.
2 Over thousands of years, the water wears the soft rock away.
3 This leaves a little step of hard rock. Which gets bigger ... and bigger until...
4 ...the raging river plunges over the edge. Splash!

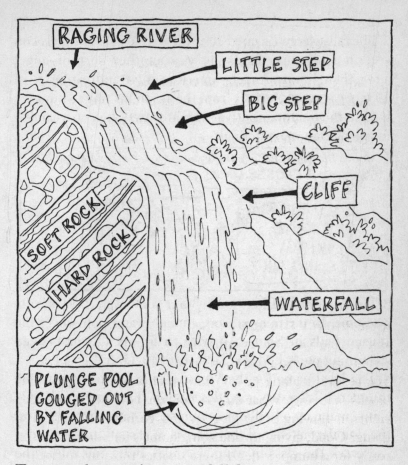

RAGING RIVER

LITTLE STEP

BIG STEP

CLIFF

SOFT ROCK

HARD ROCK

WATERFALL

PLUNGE POOL GOUGED OUT BY FALLING WATER

Ten mouth-watering waterfall facts

1 Think of a building ten storeys high. Then times it by 27. That's how high Angel Falls are and that's a world waterfall record. Angel Falls are the world's highest waterfall. Here, the River Churun plunges 979 metres down the side of Devil's Mountain in Venezuela. *Splashhhhhh!* Big waterfalls often don't wait for land to be slowly eroded so that they can trickle on downwards. They simply plunge off the edge into a valley or gorge below.

2 The falls weren't named after the rosy-cheeked angels you see on Christmas cards. It was another sort of angel altogether. Jimmy Angel, American pilot and explorer. In 1935, he spotted the falls from the air on his way to hunt for gold in the mountains. To get a better view, he crash-landed his plane right next to them!

3 The amount of water flowing over some waterfalls is truly awesome. In the rainy season, enough water pours over the Iguacu Falls in South America to fill six Olympic-sized swimming pools EVERY SINGLE SECOND!

4 The local name for the Victoria Falls is "the smoke that thunders". It's a very good description. The smoke's actually a mist made up of trillions of miniscule water droplets. And the thunderous roar of the water is so ear-splittingly loud it can crack the glass in windows miles away. You'll find the falls on the River Zambezi in Africa but don't forget your earplugs. Pardon?

5 Compared to Angel Falls, which are 20 times higher, Niagara Falls in North America is small fry. But size isn't everything. This is the most famous waterfall in the world. Everyone wants to take its picture. It's actually two falls on the Niagara River – the Horseshoe Falls on the Canadian side and the American Falls in the USA. They're separated by Goat Island.

6 Little by little, the world's waterfalls are wearing themselves out as they erode the rocks they splash over. And popular Niagara's no exception. Over the past 12,000 years, it's already gone backwards by 11 whole kilometres. Don't panic, there's still time to visit the Falls. At this rate, horrible geographers reckon, it will take the river another 25,000 years to get back to its source in Lake Erie. Then the Falls will be finished. Shame.

7 It won't be the first time the Falls have failed. In 1969, the American Falls dried up completely. But this time it was done deliberately. Experts were worried that the Falls were crumbling and they needed to get in and plug the gaps in the rock. They're back to full flow now (the Falls, you fool, not the experts).

8 Niagara gets millions of visitors. You can gawp at the Falls from Goat Island, brave them from below by boat or take the elevator to the Cave of Winds hidden behind all the falling water. Prepare to get soaked to the skin.

9 If you're feeling really brave, how about going right over the top and riding over the Falls in a barrel? That's what American teacher, Anna Edson Taylor did. On 24 October 1901, she strapped herself into a large wooden barrel and plunged over the edge. Talk about making a splash! Amazingly, apart from a few cuts and bruises, she wasn't seriously hurt. If you were thinking of getting your own teacher to give it a go, bad luck. All dangerous stunts were banned in 1911.

10 Intrepid Miss Taylor was just one of many brave (or barking mad) souls who tried to cross the Falls in weird and wonderful ways.

The barmiest was fearless Frenchman, Jean-François Gravelet (1824–1897), better known as the great Blondin (it means "Blondie").Want to read all about his daredevil adventures? We've looked in our records and dug out an old copy of *The Daily Globe* to fill you in on the story.

The Daily Globe

20 August 1859, Niagara Falls

HIGH-WIRE HIGH JINKS AT NIAGARA

Cheering crowds lined Niagara Falls yesterday to witness a truly death-defying feat. In front of thousands of nervous onlookers, the world famous acrobat, Blondin, walked across the Falls on a tightrope … carrying his manager, Mr Harry Colcord, on his back! Even though Mr Colcord was almost twice his weight!

ROOM FOR ONE MORE ON TOP

Mr Colcord was later heard to say, "Never again! It was a nightmare from beginning to end. That bloomin' Blondin nearly lost his balance at least six times! From now on, I'm keeping my feet firmly on the ground!" He wasn't the only one to have suffered a fright. Several spectators were so shocked they fainted.

This is not the first time that brave Blondin has performed his daring stunt. He made his first tightrope crossing early this year on a rope stretched 50 metres above the raging waters. On that occasion, his hair-raising hike took just under 20 minutes including a stop for a glass or two of wine. He enjoyed it so much, he came back for more.

Blondin crossed the Falls several more times, once blindfolded and once pushing a passenger along in a wheelbarrow.

ALONG FOR THE RIDE

When asked if he was ever scared, he replied, "Non (no). My father taught me how to walk ze tightrope when I was five years old. I've been doing crazy zings ever since. It is no more to me than a stroll down the Champs-Elysées."*

After this latest crossing, our on-the-spot reporter managed to snatch a few words with Blondin before he was mobbed by his adoring fans. He asked him if he'd be having another go. "Bien sûr (Of course)," Blondin replied, "I shall be back. And ze next time, I'm hoping to cross ze tightrope on stilts." Well, everyone at *The Daily Globe* wishes him bonne chance (good luck)!

* The Champs-Elysées is a famous street in Paris.

Treading a very fine line

His high jinx at Niagara earned Blondin fame and fortune, though some people had their doubts. The newpapers of the time (though not our own *Daily Globe*!) called him "a fool who ought to be arrested". But Blondin braved it out. He hadn't done badly for someone who'd started his career as a child star called the Little Wonder. But it didn't stop with stilts. In all, he crossed the Falls 17 times. Without ever falling off! Once, he stopped half way, sat down on the rope, got out a small stove and, cool as a cucumber, cooked himself an omelette! Oh well, you know what they say, food always tastes better outdoors!

Lightening the load

After all the excitement, it's high time to slow things down a bit and return to our raging river. Except it's not quite the force it used to be. It's slower and hasn't enough energy to lug its load any longer. So it dumps it at its big mouth. If the tides are strong enough, some of the load's washed out to sea. But some of it builds up into new land. The river has to branch out to flow round it, turning the river mouth into a massive maze of streams and islands called a delta. Time to dazzle your teacher with some in-depth delta data…

APPARENTLY HER CLASS KNEW MORE THAN SHE DID

Deltas were given their name by a horrible Ancient Greek historian called Herodotus. He spent a lot of his time travelling around Egypt taking notes for his new book. And one thing he noticed was that the mouth of the River Nile was triangular-shaped, a bit like the Greek letter D, or delta, which the Ancient Greeks wrote like this Δ. And the triangle thing has stuck. But you know horrible geographers. They're always meddling. So now they've come up with three delta shapes:

1 Bow shaped. The posh Latin name for this is arcuate (ark-you-ate) which means arched or bent like a bow. Officially, this is the shape of the Nile delta. Unofficially, the Ancient Egyptians said their delta was shaped like a lotus blossom. Lovely!

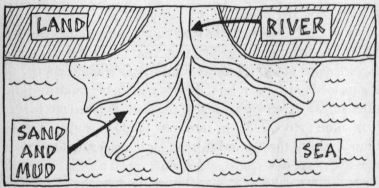

2 Pointy. The posh Latin name for this is cuspate which means shaped like a point or a peak. Remember Romulus, Remus and the bloody story of Rome? Well, the River Tiber (which Rome stands on) ends up in a pointy delta.

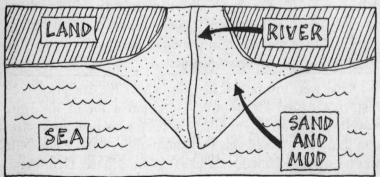

3 Bird's foot. Doesn't have a posh Latin name but you can guess its shape. It has lots of branches which look like the toes on a bird's foot. The Mississippi delta is this shape.

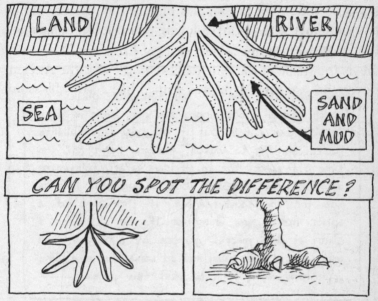

Some deltas are mind-bogglingly big. The delta of the River Ganges is gigantic, almost as big as England and Wales put together. And talking of BIG, one of the islands in the Amazon delta is about the same size as Switzerland. Some deltas are still growing. Each year, the Mississippi River dumps almost 500 million tonnes of mud and sand at its delta, pushing it further and further out to sea. As you saw on your tour, all this land is fabulously rich and fertile, so it's great for growing fruit and veg. But people living on big deltas run a big risk. Because the land's so flat and low-lying, it quickly goes under if the river floods.

Not all rivers end up in the sea. Some flow into lakes. Even more extraordinary, the Okavango River in Africa sinks into the Kalahari Desert sands. Sounds a bit dry? It's all change in the rainy season when the river floods. Then the desert delta becomes a maze of steamy swamps and sleepy lagoons, lined with tall tangles of reeds. A perfect hiding place for thousands of river-loving animals like fish eagles, hippos and crocodiles.

And me! It's one of my favourite places on Earth, though those hippos can play havoc if they capsize your canoe. But if it's wild river wildlife you're wanting to watch, and you can't get the time off school for an African safari, follow me into the next chapter. But be warned. This is not for the faint-hearted. If the sight of a spider makes you shiver or if you stand on a chair at the merest glimpse of a mouse, you may want to go away and do something else, like your homework, for the next few pages...

Rivers are wonderful places for watching wildlife. But are they such great places for wildlife to live? For hundreds of river plants and animals, raging river living isn't all plain sailing. A river is a horribly risky place to live. For a start, it depends which bit of the river you choose to live in…

Beginning
The water's cold and fast-flowing and there's not much to eat. But there's plenty of oxygen to breathe in the bubbling water (provided the current doesn't knock you off your feet).

Middle
The river's flowing more slowly now so water plants can take root in its sandy bottom. Bugs hide their ugly mugs among the plants, until they're snapped up by hungry fish.

BURP!

End

The river's slow and sluggish and the water's warmer. In some places, it's almost slowed to a halt. This is great for animals like water beetles that usually live in still-water ponds. They feel right at home.

Creature features

What do you need to survive a tiring day at school? Several cans of pop? A few bags of crisps? A long snooze through double geography? Just like you, river creatures need certain things to survive. (Come to think of it, you need all of these things too.) They are:

• Oxygen to breathe
• Food to eat
• A way of getting from A to B
• A safe place to shelter (or at least something to hang on to).

So how on Earth do they do it? Many creatures have special features to help them. Some are stranger than others. Some are downright dippy. To find out more, why not try this queasy quiz.

Dead or Alive?

We've given the creatures on the next page special features to help them survive in the river. If you think they are true, say ALIVE! If you think they are false, say DEAD! Think hard. It could be a matter of life or death.

1 Fish carry oxygen in tanks on their backs. DEAD OR ALIVE?

2 Matamata turtles breathe through snorkels. DEAD OR ALIVE?

3 The archer fish uses a bow and arrow to shoot its food. DEAD OR ALIVE?

4 Caddis fly larvae catch their food in nets. DEAD OR ALIVE?

5 Some fish love eating poo. DEAD OR ALIVE?

6 Some worms spend their whole lives with their heads in the sand. DEAD OR ALIVE?

7 Catfish cling on to rocks with their lips. DEAD OR ALIVE?

8 Dippers are birds that hate the water. DEAD OR ALIVE?

Answers:

1 DEAD! Fish breathe oxygen dissolved in the water, not tucked away in tanks on their backs. But they don't breathe through lungs like you or me. Instead they have slitty gills on the sides of their heads. You know how fish make funny popping noises with their mouths? (Open and close your mouth quickly and you'll get the idea.) This shows that they're still breathing. As the fish swims along, it closes its gills, opens its mouth and gulps in water. Then it closes its mouth, opens its gills and pushes the water out over them. Oxygen from the water goes into the fish's blood. Simple.

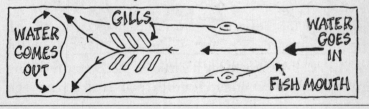

2 ALIVE! The matamata turtle lurks on the bottom of muddy rivers but, not being a fish, it needs to breathe oxygen from the air. So it sticks its long neck up out of the water so its nostrils and mouth can reach for air. This way it can also snap up passing fish before they notice it's there! Cunning.

UP PERISCOPE

3 DEAD! Archer fish don't use bows and arrows but they do have a cunning trick up their fins. They shoot down air-borne insects and insects feeding on vegetation above the water's surface with a well-aimed … glob of spit! Don't try this at home, kids!

4 ALIVE! Caddis fly larvae, or bugs, live in fast-flowing rivers where there isn't much food to go round. But this isn't a problem for these ugly bugs. They spin weeny webs between two pebbles and wait for tiny, tasty creatures to be swept downstream for dinner.

5 ALIVE! I'm sorry to say it's true. In fact, many revolting river creatures eat other creatures' poo. It all starts when dead leaves fall in the river from overhanging trees. They're crunched up by creatures like caddis fly larvae and crayfish. And it's their faeces (that's the posh word for poo) that our foul fish love to feast on.

6 ALIVE! Tubifex worms spend their whole lives with their heads in the mud on the river bottom. Why? Well, they sift food from the mud with their mouths and wave their tails about to collect oxygen. They just do it upside down. Weird or what!

7 ALIVE! Getting a grip in a fast-flowing river can be difficult at the best of times. Many creatures have hooks or suckers for holding on to slippery rocks. But catfish have a crazier way of coping. They give the rock a great big sloppy kiss and hang on with their luscious lips!

8 DEAD! Dippers love water, the faster the better. Otherwise, they'd starve. This dippy bird lives on larvae. To catch its supper, it dives underwater then walks along the river bottom flicking its wings to keep its balance and picking its food off the rocks. Its thick, oily feathers keep it warm and waterproof.

That's all very well, I hear you say, but isn't it a teeny bit tame? I mean, spitting fish and bashful worms are fine if you like that sort of thing. But it's kids' stuff. What about something meaner and moodier? OK, if you're sure... For the wettest, wildest wildlife in water, head for the awesome River Amazon. But be careful. Some of the creatures you're about to meet can turn nasty. Very nasty. Especially if they haven't had their lunch. Still keen to go? Well, don't say I didn't warn you.

Raging river fact file

NAME: River Amazon
LOCATION: South America
LENGTH: 6,400 km
SOURCE: Andes Mountains, Peru
DRAINS: 7,050,000 sq km
MOUTH: Flows into the Atlantic Ocean in Brazil
FLOW FACTS:

• It's the biggest river on Earth with the most water.
• It's got at least 1000 known tributaries (and there may be many more waiting to be found out).
• It's home to at least 1,500 types of fish. That's ten times more than in all the rivers in Europe put together! And more than in the entire Atlantic.
• The world's largest rainforest grows along its banks.

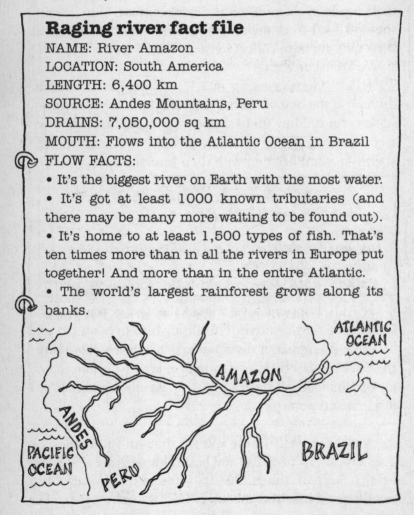

Some Amazonian animals to avoid

Travis here. I'm glad I caught you before you left. If you're determined to attempt this foolhardy adventure, I won't try to stop you. But at least let me put you in the picture. I've been helping the police with their enquiries about tracking down the most dangerous Amazonian animals. Here are my own secret files on the worst culprits. Read and digest, before they digest you!

Name: ELECTRIC EEL

Description: A knife-shaped fish, 2m long. A very sharp character.

Known Crimes: Attacking and killing unsuspecting fish and frogs (and humans).

Methods Used: Now this bit's really shocking, the eel zaps its prey with electricity (made in its tail). The shock only lasts a second but it takes the eel an hour to recharge its batteries.

Known Enemies: None really. It sees off predators in the same shocking way.

Eyewitness Account:

> I do not remember having ever received a more dreadful shock. I was affected during the rest of the day with a violent pain in my knees and almost every joint.

Alexander Von Humboldt, Scientist 1769-1859

Name: ANACONDA

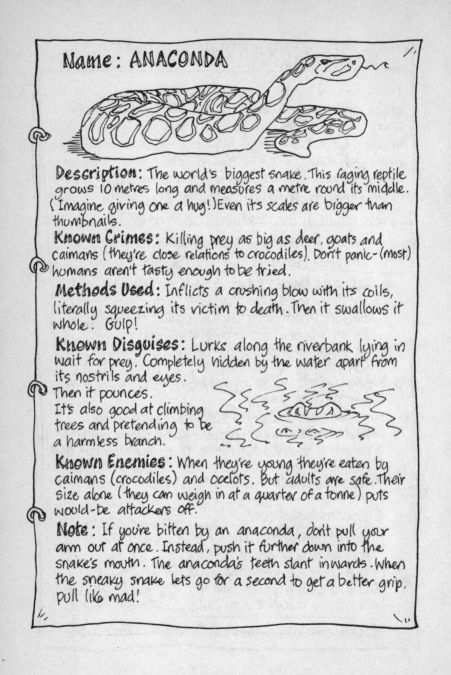

Description: The world's biggest snake. This raging reptile grows 10 metres long and measures a metre round its middle. (Imagine giving one a hug!) Even its scales are bigger than thumbnails.

Known Crimes: Killing prey as big as deer, goats and caimans (they're close relations to crocodiles). Don't panic - (most) humans aren't tasty enough to be tried.

Methods Used: Inflicts a crushing blow with its coils, literally squeezing its victim to death. Then it swallows it whole. Gulp!

Known Disguises: Lurks along the riverbank lying in wait for prey. Completely hidden by the water apart from its nostrils and eyes. Then it pounces. It's also good at climbing trees and pretending to be a harmless branch.

Known Enemies: When they're young they're eaten by caimans (crocodiles) and ocelots. But adults are safe. Their size alone (they can weigh in at a quarter of a tonne) puts would-be attackers off.

Note: If you're bitten by an anaconda, don't pull your arm out at once. Instead, push it further down into the snake's mouth. The anaconda's teeth slant inwards. When the sneaky snake lets go for a second to get a better grip, pull like mad!

Name: PIRANHA

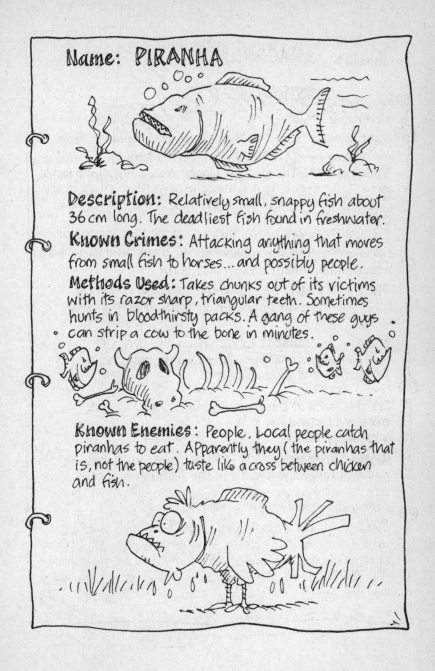

Description: Relatively small, snappy fish about 36 cm long. The deadliest fish found in freshwater.

Known Crimes: Attacking anything that moves from small fish to horses... and possibly people.

Methods Used: Takes chunks out of its victims with its razor sharp, triangular teeth. Sometimes hunts in bloodthirsty packs. A gang of these guys can strip a cow to the bone in minutes.

Known Enemies: People. Local people catch piranhas to eat. Apparently they (the piranhas that is, not the people) taste like a cross between chicken and fish.

Are you be brave enough to try your hand at a spot of piranha fishing?

What you need:
- a bow and arrow
- some poison from the skin of an arrow-poison frog. To make your own, you'll need to catch a frog. Be careful not to touch it with your bare hands – wrap them in leaves, that's what the locals do. Then stick it on a skewer and roast it over a fire so the poison's squeezed out. Alternatively, ask a local hunter (nicely) for some poison. Just a drop will do – that's more than enough to kill a whole shoal of fish!

- a watertight canoe

What you do:
1 Dip the arrow in the frog poison.
2 Paddle out into the middle of the river.

3 Take aim and ... fire.

4 Mind your fingers as you pull the fish in.

Recipe idea: To make freaky fish fingers, dip the piranhas in batter and lightly fry. Don't eat the teeth.

Note: There are some people who say that piranhas have had a very raw deal and don't deserve their ravenous reputation. They claim that they're actually rather friendly fish who prefer a snack of fruit and veg. Pah! I bet they'd be the first to run a mile if a piranha suggested a poolside barbeque!

One man who would probably have given his right arm for a freshly cooked piranha fish finger was one-eyed Spanish soldier and explorer, Francisco de Orellana (about 1490–1546). In fact, anything tasty to eat would have done very nicely. Get your teeth into this terrible tale of how fishy Francisco became the first European to sail all the way down the River Amazon, quite by accident, and largely on an empty stomach!

Up the Amazon without a paddle, sometime in 1540–1541

The Spanish had arrived in South America in 1540 with one thing on their mind – GOLD! They weren't interested in rivers or wildlife. No. They wanted to get rich quick. And they didn't care how they did it. Their greedy leader was a man called Gonzalo Pizarro who happened to be Francisco's cousin. After weeks of marching, with not a gold nugget in sight, they finally reached the River Napo, exhausted and … ravenously hungry. They'd polished off their food rations, followed by their horses, pigs and hunting dogs. Now there was hardly anything left to eat. So Pizarro sent Francisco and 50 soldiers off in search of fresh supplies. "And don't be long," he told them, having to raise his voice over the sound of his rumbling tummy. "I'm starving." Guess what? He never saw them again.

Francisco didn't mean to leave his cousin in the lurch. Well, not at first. He really meant to stock up and sail back. Honest. Or so he said. But after a week in a bumpy old boat, he didn't have the stomach for the return journey. Who says blood is thicker than water? Instead, he and his men carried on rowing and stumbled on an enormous river. It was so huge they thought at first it must be the sea. In fact, they had found the Amazon. By following the river, they reckoned they'd eventually reach the Atlantic Ocean and from there they'd sail for Spain. Home, sweet home.

Getting to the Atlantic wasn't all plain sailing. For a start, they had no idea of the length of the awesome Amazon. It just seemed to go on and on. And the local people weren't always pleased to see them. No wonder – when forceful Francisco wanted supplies, he simply captured a village and helped himself. There was plenty of time to think of a name for the river. But what to choose? In the end, he called it after a band of wild women warriors he claimed had attacked them with bows and arrows. They reminded him of the fierce female fighters of Greek legend called the Amazons.

(Oddly enough, no one else ever saw them so no one could say if he was right or wrong.) Anyway, to cut a long river short, 4,750 kilometres and eight months later, the Spaniards finally reached the sea.

What became of fearless Francisco when he got home? Was he in deep trouble for doing the dirty on his friends? Not a bit of it. His adventures were thought so exciting that the king let him off the hook. In fact, Francisco was promoted and sent back to the Amazon to claim the land for Spain. But he never made it. After all he'd been through – the heat, the flies, fiery "Amazons" – his ship went and capsized at the mouth of the river, and he drowned.

As for poor old Pizarro (remember him?), well, he waited for weeks for cousin Francisco to return. When it finally dawned on him that they weren't going to show up, he and his men hungrily began to retrace their steps to the city of Quito in Ecuador. By this time, they'd been reduced to a desperate diet of snakes, insects and even their own leather belts and saddles, boiled in water flavoured with herbs. Mmm, chewy. Of the 350 men who first set out, so many had starved to death, dropped through disease or ended up as dinner for alligators and jaguars that only 80 made it back to Quito.

Earth-shattering fact
Everything about the Amazon is larger-than-life. Take water lilies, for instance. Forget the titchy things you see floating in your dad's garden pond. These leaves are LARGE, with a capital L.A.R.G.E. Plenty large enough for your little sister to lounge about on. Don't worry about her falling in – the leaves are full of spaces which fill with air (like leafy balloons) and keep the leaf bobbing upright in the water. (Oh, you weren't worried, sorry!) Sharp thorns underneath stop the leaves being nibbled by passing fish and getting a pesky puncture!

Get wet gardening

If you're planning on planting up your own river and don't know which fluvial foliage to choose, look no further. Help is at hand with our very own green-fingered guide to riverside gardening. And if you can't tell your weeds from your water lilies, who better to turn to for advice than Travis's very own Auntie Flo.

PAPYRUS

DESCRIPTION: A TALL GRASS-LIKE PLANT. INCREDIBLY USEFUL. THE ANCIENT EGYPTIANS MADE PAPYRUS PAPER, MATS, SANDALS AND SAILS. IT'S ALSO GOOD FOR FUEL.

POSITION: SWAMPY GROUND ALONG THE RIVERBANK.

A LOVELY LOOKING PLANT THIS, AND IF YOU LEAVE IT ALONE IT'LL GROW VERY FAST, BUT DON'T LET THE SOIL GET TOO DRY. IT'S ALMOST DIED OUT IN EGYPT BECAUSE SO MUCH WATER'S BEEN DRAINED FROM THE NILE.

MANGROVE

DESCRIPTION: A LARGE, EVERGREEN TREE WITH LONG, TANGLED ROOTS SPROUTING FROM ITS TRUNK WHICH ANCHOR IT IN THE MUD. OTHER ROOTS SUCK IN AIR TO BREATHE.

POSITION: ALONG THE MOUTHS OF SOME TROPICAL RIVERS.

YOU MIGHT THINK ALL THESE ROOTS WOULD BE A MENACE. BUT THEY'RE BRILLIANT FOR PROTECTING COASTS FROM STORMS AND STOPPING THE SOIL BEING WASHED AWAY. THEY ALSO MAKE LOVELY SHELTERED SPOTS FOR FINDING FISH AND SHELLFISH.

LOOKS VERY PRETTY BUT A REAL PEST. IT SPREADS LIKE WILDFIRE AND BEFORE YOU KNOW IT, YOUR RIVER'S CLOGGED. ALMOST IMPOSSIBLE TO GET RID OF, THOUGH PEOPLE HAVE TRIED ALL SORTS OF THINGS. THEY'VE EVEN GOT WEEVILS (BUGS) INTO EAT IT AWAY BUT THEY COULD ONLY EAT SO MUCH. TO BE WEEDED OUT AT ALL COSTS.

WATER HYACINTH

DESCRIPTION: A TYPE OF WATER FERN WITH LARGE LEATHERY GREEN LEAVES AND BIG PURPLE FLOWERS.

POSITION: FLOATS ON THE SURFACE OF SOME RIVERS AND LAKES IN GREAT THICK MATS.

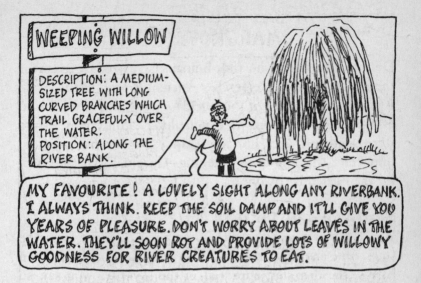

WEEPING WILLOW

DESCRIPTION: A MEDIUM-SIZED TREE WITH LONG CURVED BRANCHES WHICH TRAIL GRACEFULLY OVER THE WATER.
POSITION: ALONG THE RIVER BANK.

MY FAVOURITE! A LOVELY SIGHT ALONG ANY RIVERBANK. I ALWAYS THINK. KEEP THE SOIL DAMP AND IT'LL GIVE YOU YEARS OF PLEASURE. DON'T WORRY ABOUT LEAVES IN THE WATER. THEY'LL SOON ROT AND PROVIDE LOTS OF WILLOWY GOODNESS FOR RIVER CREATURES TO EAT.

But peckish piranhas, shocking eels and whopping great water lilies aren't the only weird wildlife you'll find near rivers. There's something far stranger lurking among the water weeds. What's that? Horrible humans, of course! Read about them in the next chapter.

Despite the dangers, horrible humans have lived by rivers for thousands of years. Remember Ancient Rome-by-the river? It's not alone. Some of the world's oldest towns, cities and even whole civilizations were built along raging rivers. Rivers were, and still are, horribly important for humans. So important that the time-watching Ancient Egyptians even set their calendar by one...

Setting a date for it

The Egyptians usually worked out their calendar from the stars. One star, in particular. The year began in June when Sirius, the dog star, appeared in the sky. OK, you say, so maybe they were top astronomers but what on Earth has all this got to do with rivers? Well, Sirius also marked the start of the River Nile's yearly flood. This happened when heavy spring rain and melting snow upriver in the mountains of Ethiopia poured massive amounts of water into the Nile. By June, the flow had reached Egypt. When the water went down, it left lots of lovely, thick, crumbly black soil behind which the green-fingered Egyptians grew bumper crops in.

But the river was more than a handy way of remembering to invite your friends round for a New Year's Eve party. It was vital to life in Ancient Egypt. You see Ancient Egypt was mostly dry, dusty desert where, green fingers or not, nothing would grow. Without the reviving River Nile, there would have been no food to eat, no water to drink, no way of travelling to visit your relatives, no relatives to visit, and no horrible Ancient Egyptian history to learn...

To see just how much the Egyptians relied on their remarkable river, try turning back the clocks. Imagine you're an Egyptian farmer. Why not call yourself Hapi (for boys) or Anukis (for girls) to help you feel the part?

Good choices if I may say so. Hapi was the god of flooding. Anukis was the goddess of the First Cataract (a series of rapids) on the Nile.

Here's what a year in your life might have been like:

1 June–October: the river floods

The raging river's in full flood now and your fields are under water. You hire the fields from a wealthy landlord who takes a cut of your crops. Luckily for you, they're right by the edge of the river, the best place for them to be. Too far back and the flood might not reach them. But the flood puts a stop to farming. Time to put your feet up for a bit? No way. During the flood, the government sends ordinary farmers like you off to help build pyramids and tombs for the king.

I WISH I WAS BACK ON THE FARM!

2 October–March: get those seeds sown

You're back from the building site and the floods are falling. Before you know it, it's all go down on the farm. You plough your fields with your wooden plough, pulled by two faithful oxen. If you're very poor, you'll have to pull the plough yourself. Then you sow handfuls of seed in the rich river soil and get ready for a non-stop round of weeding and watering. It's back-breaking work.

I WISH HE WAS BACK ON THE BUILDING SITE!

3 March–June: bring in the harvest before going back to 1

Time to sharpen your sickle (a long knife made from flintstone) and set about harvesting your crops. The taxman will be here soon to work out how much you can keep for yourself and pay to your landlord, and how much you owe to the king. If you can't pay up, you'll be beaten. And before you snatch a well-earned rest, don't forget to patch up the canals which carry water from the river into your fields. Otherwise, you'll be left high and dry.

Teacher teaser

Send your teacher into a rage with this excuse for missing double geography:

SORRY, SIR I'VE GOT TO CHECK UP ON MY NILOMETER

What on Earth are you going to do?

The Nile doesn't flood anymore because of the awesome Aswan Dam which now keeps the flow in check. The good news is that Egypt no longer gets devastatingly destructive floods. The bad news is that no more floods means no more free rich black soil.

So farmers have to fork out for chemical fertilizers to refresh their tired fields. Not only are these costly, they can poison the river water. It's a watered–down blessing.

River living – the watery truth
Despite the changes, some 50 million people still rely on the Nile for keeping them alive. And they're not the only ones. Millions of people all over the world depend on life-saving rivers. So why on Earth do they do it? Why is river living all the rage? What do rivers have to offer that you don't get from dry land? Some people rave on about the views. Others rant about finding rivers relaxing. But the real reason why humans live near raging rivers is … raging river water.

Wonderful water

How much water do you use in a day? You've probably never given it a second thought. Well, prepare to be amazed. The answer is a lavish 150 litres. That's about the same as two big bathtubsful or 600 cans of pop!

Here are just some of the things you can do with all this horrible H_2O. You can:

• **Drink it**. Water is absolutely vital for life. Without it, you'd literally die of thirst in a few days. But did you know that most drinking water comes from raging rivers? If you want a thirst-quenching glass of water, you simply turn on the tap. But how on Earth did the water get there in the first place? Here's how you get water on tap:

1 A dam is built across a river...

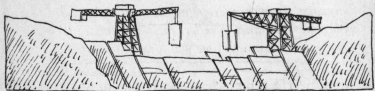

2 ...forming a big lake called a reservoir.

3 The water's piped from here to the waterworks where it's cleaned and made safe to drink.

4 First, the water flows through a screen to filter out twigs, leaves and branches.

5 Then it soaks through a bed of fine sand to filter out any dirt.

6 A gas called chlorine's added to kill any germs.

7 Then the clean water's piped underground and through smaller pipes into your home.

- **Wash in it.** Keeping clean uses hundreds of litres of river water a day. You use about 80 litres every time you have a bath, 10 litres when you flush the toilet and about 100 litres for every load in the washing machine.

a) Have a shower instead of a bath. It'll save about 50 litres of water. (Of course, skipping both saves even more but you might end up ponging a bit.)

b) Don't leave the tap running when you clean your teeth. (But don't forget to keep brushing twice a day.)

c) Put half a brick in your toilet cistern. (Ask permission first!) It'll cut down the water you use to flush the loo by about a third. (Don't worry, it'll still do the job.)

• **Water your fields with it.** Farming is horribly thirsty work. Growing a 1 kilogram bag of rice uses 35 bathtubs of water! Goodness knows how much bathwater it took to cook your school dinner. Some of the richest farmland in the world lies around river deltas where there's always a good water supply. Take the delta of the River Mekong in Vietnam. It's like a gigantic rice field where half the country's rice is grown. Sometimes the water needs a helping hand. It's pumped and sprinkled on fields, brought by canal or is even controlled by computer. The posh name for this is irrigation.

The Ancient Egyptians knew all about irrigation. They used an ingenious device called a shaduf to freshen up their fields. It was simple but brilliant. In fact, it worked so well that it's still going strong today. Are you nimble-fingered enough to make your own full-sized shaduf?

What you need:
- three strong canes about 1.5 metres long
- one strong cane about 1.75 metres long
- some rope or strong string
- one small bucket
- a carrier bag of sand (Note: to decide how big the bag needs to be, fill the bucket with water. The bag needs to weigh the same.)
- a strong adult to help you

What you do:

1 Tie the three canes together to make a tepee shape.

2 Stand your tepee firmly in the ground.

3 Tie the middle of the longer cane to the top of the tepee. This cane becomes the lever.

4 Tie your bucket to one end...

5 ...and your bag of sand to the other to weigh it down.

How it works:

Farmers use a shaduf to lift water from the river into their fields. First they push the weighted end up to lower the bucket into the water. Then they pushed it down to raise the full bucket. Simple, eh! This means that one farmer can lift thousands of litres of water on his own, in a day. It's much quicker and easier than filling buckets by hand (and saves all that bending over). Don't forget to ask permission before you try out your shaduf on your dad's prize-winning veg!

- **Catch your dinner in it.**

1 Forget high-tech fishing boats, full of mod cons. Forget fishing rods, hooks and lines. Try fishing the River Amazon way. There, fishermen beat the water with bundles of vines until their poisonous juice oozes out. This kills the fish and they float to the surface where they're scooped up in baskets and nets. Cunning!

2 You'd need a basket the size of a small boat to catch a pirarucu. It's the biggest river fish. It lives in the Amazon and weighs a whopping 200 kilograms. That's over four times heavier than you! People eat it dried or salted. Apparently it tastes a bit like cod.

3 If you can't get to a river, bring a river into your home. Some farmers in the Mekong River delta keep catfish under the living room floor! Their houses are built on stilts over the river. Every day, they open a trapdoor in the floor and feed the fish to fatten them up for market. (Don't try this at home, kids. Stick to goldfish instead!)

• **Light up your house with it.** Next time you turn on the light, think about where all that electricity comes from. The answer might be, you've guessed it, a river. About a fifth of all our electricity comes from raging rivers. It's cheap, clean and it won't run out. To get at it, you need a raging river and a dam. As the water flows through the dam, it turns the blades of a wheel called a turbine. In turn it drives a shaft which drives a generator to generate electricity.

Got it? Technically it's called hydro-electricity (hydro means water). It's best if the river's raging downhill, so Niagara Falls is really humming.

• **Run your factory with it**. How much water does it take to make a car? Go on, have a guess, it's not a trick question. The answer is about 50 bathtubsful. That's how much water a steelworks uses to make a car's worth of steel. Factories need huge amounts of water to turn raw materials into the goods we use. It's used for processing the materials. This means cleaning them, mixing them and cooling them down. That's why many factories are built near rivers so they can use the water. Take the raging River Rhine for example...

Raging river fact file

NAME: River Rhine
LOCATION: Central Europe
LENGTH: 1,390 km
SOURCE: Two small streams in the Swiss Alps
DRAINS: 220,000 sq km
MOUTH: Flows into the North Sea near Rotterdam in Holland
FLOW FACTS:

● Because it runs right across the heart of Europe, through many leading industrial countries, it's the busiest river in the world. There's a constant stream of tugs and barges carrying steel, iron ore, coal, timber, petrol and other heavy cargoes.

● Rotterdam is the world's busiest seaport. Each year, it handles about 300 million tonnes of cargo and about 30,000 ships dock there.

● The River Ruhr is a tributary of the Rhine. Its banks are lined with hundreds of factories making chemicals, iron, steel, cars and computers.

Messing about on the river

Anything else you can do with a raging river? Mess about on it, of course. (Be careful, though, rivers can be dangerous places.) If you're longing for a spot of fast-flowing fun, why not pay a visit to the village of Flowing-oh-so-slowly which is holding its annual sports day?

VILLAGE NEWS BOARD

The village of Flowing oh-so-slowly is proud to present its...

☆ ANNUAL RAGING RIVER SPORTS DAY ☆

Come along and make a Splash!

EVERYBODY WELCOME (what ever your watersport)

ALL WINNERS GUARANTEED A FABULOUS PRIZE

TURN THE PAGE AND CHOOSE A SPORT →

ANGLING

SEE IF YOU CAN BEAT THE WORLD RECORD FOR THE MOST FISH CAUGHT- 625 IN A DAY!

ROWING

MIND YOU DON'T CATCH A CRAB! THAT'S THE TECHNICAL TERM FOR GETTING YOUR OAR STUCK IN THE WATER

SWIMMING

DON'T GET CARRIED AWAY BY THE CURRENT!

CANOEING

DON'T GO AND CAPSIZE NOW!

WINDSURFING

CAN YOU KEEP YOUR BALANCE?

PICNICKING

BACK THIS YEAR BY POPULAR DEMAND! A SPECIAL PRIZE FOR THE MOST ORIGINAL SANDWICH. LAST YEAR'S WINNER: PIRANHA, MAYONNAISE + WATERCRESS

Are you brave enough to ride the rapids?

If it's a really raging good time you're after, why not try your luck at white-water rafting? Feeling daring? You'll need to be. White-water rafting means hurtling over obstacles like rock-hard boulders and raging rapids … in a blow-up boat! Having second thoughts? What about taking Travis along to show you how it's done?

What you need:
- a raging river
- a really tough inflatable (blow up) raft
- a paddle (single-bladed)
- a life-jacket
- a wetsuit and a crash helmet
- five other victims (sorry, volunteers) to go with you

What you do:

1 Blow up your raft by the riverbank.

2 Get into the raft. Three of you should sit on each side of the raft, right up on the sides, with Travis at the back. He's in charge of steering and shouting orders!

3 Paddle gently out into the middle of the river, then paddle straight ahead. Try to keep in time and get a nice rhythm going.

4 Rapids ahead! You need to aim for the spot with the fewest rocks. You don't want to get a puncture. If it's in the centre, Travis will tell you to keep going straight. To turn the raft to the right, keep paddling if you're on the left. To turn left, paddle if you're on the right. (Note: to brake, you all need to paddle backwards!)

5 Just before you hit the rapids, jump down into the bottom of the raft so you're not swept overboard as you bump over them. And prepare to get wet, soaking wet.

6 When (hopefully) you come out on the other side, steer the raft back to the riverbank and get out. Or, if you're feeling brave, stay in the boat and keep going to the next set of rapids…

A few more horribly helpful hints and tips:
Travis thinks he's a bit of an expert when it comes to white-water rafting, so let's see how he does – and no laughing!
• Pick your rapids carefully. They're graded on a scale of 1 to 6. Grade 6 rapids are described as "nearly impossible and very dangerous, for experts only". They're wild.

Maybe start off more gently with a Grade 2…

…or a Grade 3.

- Better still, go as part of a group and take an expert with you. They'll help you out if you run into trouble. If they don't run into trouble first…

- If you do fall in, try to swim down to the bottom of the rapids where the water's calmer. Then swim to the bank and get out. And whatever you do, keep hold of your paddle. Or you'll be well and truly up a creek without a paddle…

Don't worry if white-water rafting isn't for you. You're in good company. Sometimes even the experts get more than they'd banked on. Maybe you'd rather relax on the riverbank and read about ways of getting downriver without getting wet instead? And get to meet some real-life river rovers on the way.

RAGING RIVER ROVING

For centuries, people have used rivers to get from A to B. Forget boring cars, trains and planes. If you wanted to visit your auntie in the next town, it was quickest to go by river. Today, rivers are still used for moving people and goods about. But in many parts of the world, cars, trains and planes have well and truly taken over.

But raging river roving didn't always have an end in sight. Sometimes intrepid explorers set off up rivers without knowing where on Earth they were going. Often they hadn't a clue what lay around the next bend in the river, let alone how they'd make it home. Sometimes it was just as well not to know. So why on Earth did they do it? Sometimes they were promised a reward. But more often than not, it was simply for the sake of having an earth-shattering adventure.

Travels up the Niger

In the eighteenth century, some of London's leading horrible geographers set up an association for the study of African rivers.

I PROPOSE WE EXPLORE...HERE!

But it wasn't just geographical discovery they had in mind. They wanted to find a trade route into Africa and make some serious money. They desperately needed someone to go and explore the River Niger (everyone else they'd sent had died

114

or disappeared). And in 1795, they found the perfect volunteer – a keen, young Scottish doctor called Mungo Park (1771–1806). His mission was to track the river along its entire length from source to mouth. But first he had to find it. And that was easier said than done. Over the page is how Mungo might have described his journey in his letters to his boss, Henry Beaufoy…

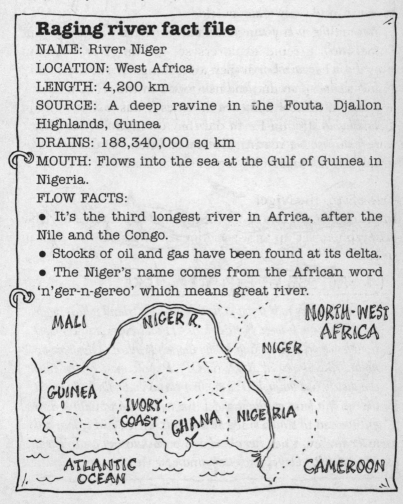

Raging river fact file

NAME: River Niger

LOCATION: West Africa

LENGTH: 4,200 km

SOURCE: A deep ravine in the Fouta Djallon Highlands, Guinea

DRAINS: 188,340,000 sq km

MOUTH: Flows into the sea at the Gulf of Guinea in Nigeria.

FLOW FACTS:

- It's the third longest river in Africa, after the Nile and the Congo.
- Stocks of oil and gas have been found at its delta.
- The Niger's name comes from the African word 'n'ger-n-gereo' which means great river.

Nightmare on the Niger

A village in Africa, 30 March 1796

Dear Mr Beaufoy,
    Thank you for your letter and the pay rise (yippee!). Fifteen shillings a day is really most generous. And it's come in the nick of time (but more of that later).

    I don't know where on earth to begin to tell you all my news. The journey from England was most pleasant. The ship was adequate, the weather fair and the crossing took just 30 days. On landing in Africa, I headed down the River Gambia, according to plan, then continued by horse overland. (I must say, I am still rather saddlesore.)

    For days we rode through flat, rolling grassland which made me pine for my beloved Scottish hills. The weather was also most troublesome. I was boiling hot by day and chilled to the bone by night. And it rained NON-STOP. I spent most of the time completely wet through. You see, my trusty umbrella had caught the eye of a local chieftain and I was forced to part with it as a gift (he wasn't a man to say no to). Still, I was looking forward to the challenges that lay ahead and to reaching my goal. Then, on Christmas Day, things took a turn for the worse.

A murderous mob of bandits attacked us and stole almost everything we owned. Right down to my waistcoat buttons! And in broad daylight! Then, to cap it all, I was arrested as a spy. Me! I've never spied on anyone in my life. I tried to talk my way out of it (you know how I pride myself on talking things through) but I ended up being clapped in the local prison.

Well, I somehow managed to give the guards the slip and make my escape but by now I had nothing but the clothes I stood up in. I was in very dire straits indeed. I don't know what would have become of me if a kindly old woman hadn't given me food though she hardly had enough for herself. (So you see, the pay rise really will come in handy.)

Luckily, the robbers didn't get their thieving fingers on my precious papers which I always keep safely tucked under my hat. You'll be pleased to hear that I've taken a great many notes about local customs (with a special chapter on prisons) which I look forward to showing you on my return. If I ever return... Until then, I shall press on with my quest

Yours sincerely,
Mungo Park

Segon, on the Niger, Mali, 20 July 1796

Dear Mr Beaufoy,
     We've found it! We've found it! And it flows eastwards, not westwards as everyone thought. How it lifted my spirits to see it glistening there in the morning sun like the good old Thames at Westminster… It's BRILLIANT! I'm sooo excited. Yippeee!

Bye for now,
Mungo Park
PS Erm, sorry. I got a bit carried away. Very embarrassing and unscientific of me. I can promise you it won't happen again.

Somewhere up the Niger, 30 July 1796

Dear Mr Beaufoy,
     That's it – I've had it. I can't carry on. I'm tired, wet, penniless and my poor old horse is a gibbering wreck.
     I tried, I really tried. But enough is enough. You see, I hadn't the money for a canoe (I was robbed again – bang goes my pay rise) so, more dead than alive, my horse and I set off upstream to find the river's mouth. But it's been ten days now, and there's no end in sight. I asked a local chap if he knew where the river flowed to. He replied rather gloomily, "To the ends of the Earth." I can well believe it.

     Yours dejectedly, Mungo Park

Exhausted, broke and bitterly disappointed, Mungo Park went home. He still had nightmares about prisons but things very quickly looked up. He wrote a best-selling book of his travels and became a household name. (Well, would you forget a name like Mungo?) And while he was back home, he met and married the lovely Alison and settled down in Scotland to live happily ever after. Actually it was only for a little while. Despite everything, Mungo couldn't get Africa out of his mind. When he was offered another nose at the Niger, he was off like a shot. But he still found time to write to his wife…

Somewhere in West Africa, 13 June 1805

My Dearest Allie,

    Half way through our journey now and things are going OK-ish, I suppose. Who am I kidding? It's been a disaster. Talk about leaving things to the last minute. It's been one delay after the other. First the soldiers sent to accompany me didn't show up (and when they did, they were a horribly bad-tempered, rowdy lot), then the supplies went missing.

    Anyway, we finally set off. I know what you're thinking, dear. The rainy season's about to begin. I must be mad to go anywhere. But what choice did I have? If we'd waited any longer, we'd never have gone at all. And the sooner we get there, the sooner we can all go home…
    Missing you dreadfully. Please don't worry. I'll be fine.

Your devoted Mungo

Sansanding, on the Niger, 17 November 1805

My dearest Allie,

    We finally reached the Niger on 19 August. I'm sorry I didn't write sooner but I've been rather busy with other things. To tell you the truth, things have been going from bad to worse. The rains made the going very soggy and slow (I know, you told me so) and very few of the men made it. I suppose a more sensible chap would have given up and gone home by now. But you know me, dear. Once I make up my mind to do something, I like to see it through to the bitter end. Call me a stubborn old fool, if you like.

    Things looked up a bit when the local chieftain promised me a couple of canoes. But they turned out to be rotten and full of holes.

    I saved what I could of the good wood and patched it together to make a boat. It's a bit leaky but it'll have to do. And now we're heading downstream. So you see, dear, the end is really and truly in sight.

    Dearest, I'm sending this letter by courier which should be quicker than boat. But I should be home long before it reaches you.

    Wish you were here, or I was there.

All my love,
Your Mungo

A watery end

If you only like stories with a happy ending, skip the next bit. This was Mungo's last letter to his wife. He was never heard from again. Only his local guide was left to fill in the gaps. According to him, Mungo sailed 2,400 kilometres down-river, fighting off enemy canoes and nosy hippos. Another 960 kilometres and he'd have reached the river's mouth and his journey's end. Then disaster struck. Mungo was ambushed by unfriendly locals. The game was up. Rather than wait to be killed, Mungo jumped into the river and was swept away.

Did he drown? Most people think so. But not everyone. For years, rumours reached Britain of a tall, red-headed man, speaking English, and living by the Niger...

As for the Africa Association who got poor Mungo into this mess in the first place, they were taken over by the British government. But this didn't stop them. They sent several more expeditions to follow in Mungo Park's footsteps. In 1830, the two Clapperton brothers set off up the Niger. People sniggered because of the way they dressed, in scarlet tunics, huge baggy trousers and enormous straw hats the size of umbrellas, but the Clappertons had the last laugh. Despite their critics, they managed to sail right down the river, right to its mouth and so finally put the River Niger well and truly on the map (though they only got a £100 reward for their pains).

River diseases

1 Malaria

Symptoms: Raging fever with a horribly high temperature. Terrible headaches, sweating and death. Especially bad in hot, swampy places.

Cause: Malarial mosquitoes which lay their eggs on the surface of slow-flowing rivers or ponds. When they hatch, they hover near the water. When they're hungry, they bite you, suck your blood and squirt deadly parasites into your veins. A parasite is a blood-thirsty creature that lives off other creatures. Nasty.

Any known cure? A course of pills usually does the trick. And of course it helps if you don't get bitten in the first place. Use mosquito repellant, cover up (particularly at dusk) and sleep under a mosquito net. An old-fashioned explorer's cure is to slap mud on your face! Well, it should take your mind off things!

2 River blindness

Symptoms: Horribly itchy skin. Damaged eyesight and in the worst cases blindness.

Cause: Blackflies which live and breed in tropical rivers. They bite you and spit tiny grubs into the wound.

Inside you, these grow into worms and lay their eggs which hatch into millions more worms. The worms spread through your body. Dead worms inside your eyes can make you go blind. Horrible.

Any known cure? A yearly dose of medicine, taken by mouth, can prevent blindness. Spraying rivers where blackflies breed helps to keep the disease at bay.

3 Bilharzia (bill-har-zi-a)

Symptoms: Itchy skin or rash, fever, chills, aches, pains and death. Can seriously damage your liver, guts, kidneys and bladder. So nothing too serious, then!

Cause: Tiny worm grubs. They live inside tropical river snails.

Then the grubs swap the snails for you. If you're in the river at the same time, the grubs can burrow through your skin and into your blood. There they lay their eggs. Yuk!

Any known cure? Yes, a simple injection or a course of pills.

Could you be a river rover?

Could you follow in Mungo Park's footsteps and become a raging river rover? Picture the scene... You've been walking for miles. You're tired, your feet hurt, you've been munched by what feels like a million mosquitoes and you just want to go home. You can see the path you need to take but, guess what? It's on the other side of a raging river!

So how on Earth do you get across? Decide which one of these methods you think would work best? Then check out the answers on pages 128–132.

1 Take a boat across it. Obvious really, but the question is what sort of boat do you choose? Take your pick from these raging river rovers.

A DUG-OUT CANOE

B FELUCCA

C JUNK

D STEAMBOAT

E FERRYBOAT

CRUISESHIP

If you go by boat, watch out for sandbars. They're big dunes of sand on the river bed, ruffled up by the current. And they're horribly hazardous. The problem is they're so hard to spot and can suddenly shift without warning. Before you know it, you'll be grounded or even sunk. Best take a pilot with you (that's an expert in navigation). He'll know the river like the back of his hand.

2 Build a bridge across it. People have been bridging the gap for thousands of years. But what have bridges been made of? Which of these is too silly to be true?

a) old logs
b) old ropes
c) old rocks
d) old human heads

3 Dig a tunnel under it. Go on, get shovelling. It's not as silly as it sounds. There are several tunnels running under the River Thames in England. The first was built to last in 1842 by British engineer Marc Brunel. It was the first underwater tunnel in history. Today tube trains race through it.

4 Swim across it. If you're a strong swimmer, take a good, deep breath and dive in. But if your doggy paddle lets you down, you might need some help. If you can't be seen dead in armbands, hold on to a floating log for support. Or do what the ancient Assyrians did and grab on to a blown-up pig's bladder instead! Before you jump in, slap on plenty of insect repellant!

5 Pole vault over it. If all else fails, you could always go and take a running jump...

Answers:

1 All these boats can be used on rivers but it depends which river you choose. For fast-flowing rivers, dug-out canoes are just the job. They're light, tough and easy to steer. But watch out for particularly strong currents. Before you know it, you'll be swept downstream. To get over the river, paddle across and slightly upstream, HARD! For busy rivers, feluccas are neat and nippy for weaving in and out of traffic. They've been used on the Nile since Ancient Egyptian times. For deep, wide rivers, why not jump on a Chinese junk. Hope you're feeling strong. If the river's too high or too low, you might have to get out and pull. But if raging river currents are a problem, you'll need a boat with an engine. You could go for a modern motorboat but a classic old steamboat would really impress your friends. They were once a frequent sight on the Mississippi but now they mostly take tourists around. Fancy a bet? Some steamboats double up as floating casinos. For very wide rivers, hop on the ferry. Most big rivers have one. But get there early. They're often the only lift around and they can get horribly crowded. And finally, for rivers with history on their side, a cruiseship's the perfect choice. If you're feeling flash, why not cruise along the River Nile. You can see all the sights without leaving your deckchair.

2 d) Of course, you don't actually get bridges *built* of heads! Most of old London Bridge across the River Thames was made of sensible stone. But it also had a row of sharp spikes at each end. And guess what was on the ends of the spikes – yes, the chopped-off heads of traitors and criminals! Gruesome!

The very first bridges were probably logs or stepping stones laid across a stream. Rope bridges are often used in the jungle, made from vines. You have to hold on tight, as they wobble a lot.

Yes, bridges are often the quickest and easiest way of crossing a river. But you'll need to choose the right type. Are you brave enough to find out how to build a bridge?

What you need:
- some logs (assorted lengths)
- some stones
- a raging river

What you do:
a) Lay a long log across the river so it reaches from one bank to the other. Congratulations! You've made a simple beam bridge and it's great for crossing a narrow river.

GOOD DOG...GO AND FETCH THE FIRE BRIGADE...

b) For a wider river, you'll need a longer log and it needs to be stronger. Otherwise it will sag in the middle as you walk across it.

c) On a very wide river, you'll need to lay several logs end to end. Put a few piles of stones in the water for the logs to rest on. Technically, these piles are called piers.

RIVER

BEAM OF LOGS

PIERS: TOPS STICK JUST ABOVE THE WATER

Note: if the river's horribly deep and wide, forget beam bridges. The logs and piers would be just too huge. Instead you'll need a suspension bridge. That's a bridge which hangs from long, steel cables suspended from tall towers. These bridges can be more than a kilometre long. And that's a job for a proper engineer!

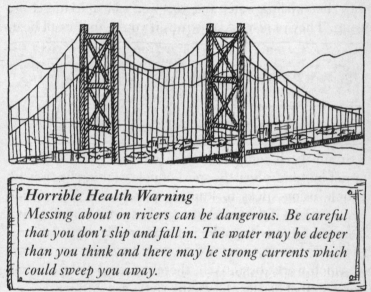

3 Tunnelling can work but be careful. Even for experts, underwater tunnels are tricky to build. Because they go under the soft riverbed rocks, their roofs and walls can easily cave in. Brunel had to design a special tunnelling machine for the job. It burrowed through the rock, holding up the roof while the workers were left to line the tunnel. Clever, eh? Especially when you know that Brunel got the idea from watching a wood-boring mollusc at work. Modern tunnelling machines are still based on Brunel's brilliant invention.

4 This is a good idea, if you can swim, though maybe leave out the pig. And watch out for weirs. They're small, low dams built across the river and they block the river to make a deep pool like a small harbour for boats. They're often hidden by the water – making them doubly dangerous. If you're swept over one, you'll get sucked into the swirling water and you won't be able to get out again. They're just as dangerous if you're in a small boat.

5 Strangely enough, you'd be in good company. Believe it or not but this is how the sport of pole vaulting began with people using sticks to leap across streams. You should easily make it if the river's narrow but get a good run up if it's wide. Otherwise you're in for a horribly soggy landing.

So, which works best? Well, there's no real right or wrong answer to that because all raging rivers are different!

Earth-shattering fact
What if the river's too narrow or shallow to take big ships? You make it deeper and wider, of course! That's what engineers did to the St Lawrence River in North America. And they tacked some canals on the end. Ships can now make the 3769-kilometre trip from the Atlantic Ocean and across the Great Lakes in just eight days. The only snag is that the waterway's blocked by ice in winter and there's nothing the engineers can do about that!

You might think that deadly diseases, life-threatening weirs and leaky canoes were the worst that the river could throw at you. But you'd be wrong, horribly wrong. So far, your river's been quite well behaved. It's true. But things are about to change. Prepare to be swept off your feet. You're about to see the other side of the river. A side you haven't seen before. When the river's true colours come flooding out...

RIVER RAGE

If you think things look bad when your teacher loses his temper, beware of a river in a rage. In a flash, a river can change completely from a nice, babbling brook to a raging torrent. If this happens to a river near you, get out of the way, fast! Furious floods can be horribly hazardous, sweeping away everything in their path. INCLUDING YOU! And the freaky thing is that they can happen anywhere, anytime…

What on Earth is a flood?

Want to find out about floods but too wet to ask? Worried about keeping your head above water? Here's Travis to throw you in at the deep end…

SO, WHAT ON EARTH IS A FLOOD THEN?

It's when a raging river overflows because it's too full of water. Simple really. Like when you fill a glass too full of pop.

HMM, I SEE, AND WHY DOES THIS HAPPEN?

Most floods happen when massive, and I mean massive, amounts of rain fall in a very short time. The river just can't cope. You also get floods when melting snow swells the river or when a dodgy dam bursts. Or when cyclones or tidal waves whip up the sea into a frenzy.

BLIMEY! WHERE DOES ALL THE OVERFLOW GO?

It spills on to the floodplain. That's the flat land on either side of the river which is normally dry. It can be a few metres across or a few hundred kilometres, and it's made of mud and sand dumped by the river.

WHY DOESN'T THE WATER JUST SOAK INTO THE GROUND? THEN IT WOULDN'T MATTER IF THE RIVER FLOODED.

Good point. But it's not as simple as that, I'm sorry to say. If the rain's very heavy, the ground can't soak it up fast enough and the soil becomes water-logged. Then any floodwater just lies on top.

AND ARE FLOODS REALLY DANGEROUS?

Yes and no. Some rivers flood every year without doing much damage. But a really fierce flood can be fatal. It can drown fields and crops, wash away buildings and cause millions of pounds of damage. And cost lives. In fact, furious floods do more damage and kill more people than any other natural disaster. And that's official! The worst flood on record happened in 1931, when the Huang He River in China burst its banks killing no less than 4 million people and leaving 80 million homeless. Horrible.

WHY DON'T PEOPLE LIVE SOMEWHERE SAFER?

Millions of people don't have much choice. They live in countries where there's already too little land to go round. Besides, the soil on the floodplain is so fantastically fertile, they're willing to run the risk.

WHICH RIVERS SHOULD I AVOID AT ALL COSTS?

Most rivers can turn nasty if conditions are right. But without doubt one of riskiest is the raging Yangtze River in China...

The Daily Globe

Sunday 2 August 1998, Hunan Province, eastern China

MILLIONS IN FEAR AS FLOOD WATERS RISE

A week after the Yangtze burst its banks for the third time in two months, millions of Chinese are still on full flood alert. Today, water levels on the river broke all previous records, leaving terrified villagers in fear of being literally washed away.

The Yangtze has been rising since spring, placing enormous pressure on the fragile system of dykes or embankments which separate the river from the 200 million people living along its banks. With floodwater now surging downstream, people are getting really very frightened.

"We're praying we can prevent a disaster," an elderly villager told our reporter. "We've been making the dykes round our village higher with mud. But if the dykes don't hold when the river comes, we'll lose everything."

DAM BUILDERS

Elsewhere in the region some dykes have already collapsed and several villages lie swamped under two metres of water. This year's floods have already claimed 2,500 lives – numbers are still rising – and driven millions of villagers out of their homes. Some have been stranded for days on their roofs, helplessly watching the unstoppable rise of the water.

ROOF TOPS

And now a new danger is lurking. Doctors are warning that disease could be the next disaster to strike. In some places, polluted floodwater has already contaminated drinking water and placed millions at risk of sickness and diarrhoea.

But getting the sick to hospital is no easy matter.

"I saw some people being rowed to hospital in boats," an eyewitness said. "But the first floor of the hospital was under water. I don't know how they got in."

So, who is to blame for the disaster? This is a question many people are asking. True, the river has been flooding for centuries but this year's torrential summer rains have made the problem much worse. Some people blame the government for not spending enough money on repairing the dykes. If they don't act soon, locals fear, the same thing will happen again and again.

"I have nothing," one farmer told us after he'd seen his home, all his belongings and his crops completely washed away. "I'll have to start all over again."

And this may not be the last time...

Raging river fact file

NAME: Yangtze River
LOCATION: China
LENGTH: 6,418 km
SOURCE: Mount Gelandandong, Tibet
DRAINS: 1,683,500 sq km
MOUTH: Flows into the East China Sea (part of the Pacific Ocean) near Shanghai.

FLOW FACTS:

● In Chinese, it's called the Chang Jiang or Long River. Legend says it was carved out by a goddess.

● It's the world's third longest river after the Nile and Amazon.

● About three-quarters of all the rice grown in China is grown on its floodplain.

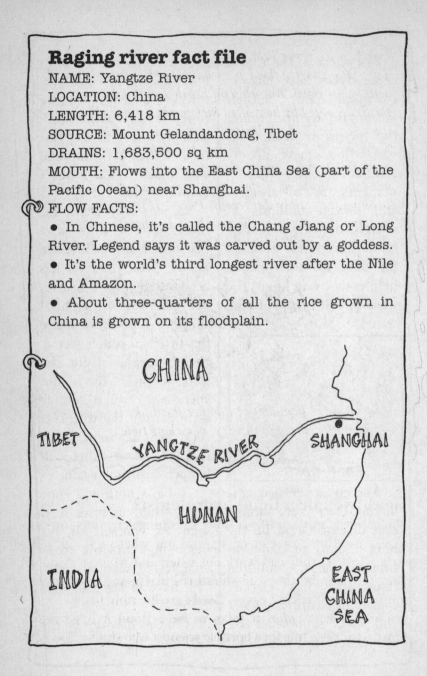

CHINA

TIBET

YANGTZE RIVER

SHANGHAI

HUNAN

INDIA

EAST CHINA SEA

The 1998 Yangtze flood was what horrible geographers call a 100-year flood. But what on Earth does this mean? Well, floods are rated by how often they might happen. The more frequent they are, the better. A one-year flood is likely to happen once a year and doesn't do much damage. A 100-year flood means that, each year, there's a one-in-a-hundred chance of a flood that can do a lot of damage. Making it horribly dangerous. Phew! If that sounds bad, imagine the horror of the people of Lynmouth, England, when a freak 50,000-year flood smashed their village to pieces in 1952.

At least there shouldn't be another flood like it (with that river, at any rate!) for a very, very long time.

Could you be a flood hydrologist?

Once a river's in full flood, there's nothing scientists can do to stop it. But they can try to find out where a flood will strike next. If they can work out when and where a flood's likely to happen, they can sound the alarm and get people out of the way. It isn't easy – floods are horribly fickle.

Do you have what it takes to be a flood hydrologist? (That's the posh title for a horrible scientist who studies floods.)

HORRIBLE JOB ADVERT

Tired of keeping your feet on the ground?
Is life driving you round the bend? Fancy
a spell in the fast stream? Why not join
our team of top hydrologists?
- You must like the outdoors and be a
strong swimmer.

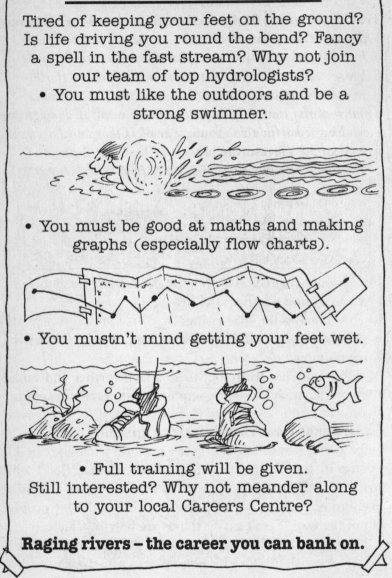

- You must be good at maths and making
graphs (especially flow charts).

- You mustn't mind getting your feet wet.

- Full training will be given.
Still interested? Why not meander along
to your local Careers Centre?

Raging rivers – the career you can bank on.

And here's Travis to show you the ropes…

Travis's (almost) fool-proof guide to flood forecasting
1 Get to know your river
You need to study your river carefully and get to know all of its twists and turns. Most importantly, you need to see how it reacts when it rains. Ask yourself these two questions:
a) How much rain is falling? You don't need loads of posh measuring gear for this. You can make a simple rain gauge from a kitchen measuring jug.

But serious scientists also scan the skies for rain using high-tech radars and weather satellites.
b) How much is the river rising? Scientists study river levels with a nifty gadget called a stream sensor. It radios back data to a computer.
c) Some hot-shot hydrologists go a step further and build their own model river, complete with fake meanders, floodplains and floods. They use this to test how the river reacts and how dams and dykes hold up against floods.

FLASH FLOOD!

2 Chart your river's progress

Next, feed all your info into a computer. It will do loads of earth-shattering equations and plot the results on a chart. (The posh name for this is a hydrograph.) (But you'll need to double check it's got things right and that's where being wicked at maths will help.) The chart will show how the river copes with rain, and how long before it overflows. From this you can work out how likely a flood is, and how long you've got to get outta there...

3 Sound the alarm

If it's raining heavily and the river's rising rapidly, for goodness' sake sound the alarm! In Britain, flood warnings are colour-coded according to the degree of risk.

- **Yellow Warning**

  Risk of flooding to low-lying farmland and roads near rivers.

- **Amber Warning**

  Risk of flooding to isolated homes and larger areas of farmland near rivers.

- **Red Warning**

  Risk of serious flooding to many properties, roads and large areas of farmland.

So how watertight was your warning? Of course, you can't tell for sure until the flood's been and gone. The trouble is that floods are horribly unpredictable. You can't always work out what they'll do next. For big rivers like the Mississippi, you might have a week's warning of flooding. But you might have just a few hours to flee from a flash flood. (That's a flood that rises incredibly quickly after an unusually heavy downpour of rain.)

Stopping the flow

You know the saying, "Prevention is better than cure"? It means that it's better to stop your teeth rotting in the first place by not eating too many sweets than to spend hours afterwards at the dentist. It's usually used about people. But the same could be said for floods. You might not be able to stop a flood in mid-flow but you can take steps to reduce the damage. How? Well, for a start, you could...

● **Plant some trees.** Here's how it works:

1 Plant leaves trap rain before it can hit the ground. In a forest, about three-quarters of rain is waylaid like this.

2 Plant roots suck up water from the soil, and also bind the soil together.

The problem is that plants and trees are being cut down for firewood or to clear farmland. And this means there's nothing to stop the rain pouring into the river. The rain also washes away loads of loose soil which raises the river bed so it floods more easily.

● **Change the shape of the river.** Try making the river straighter, wider and deeper. It'll work wonders. It makes it easier for the river to flow so it reaches the sea faster without overflowing. But you'll need a special digging machine called a dredger.

● **Change the river's course.** By building a ditch or channel to divert the water away. It's also useful for storing spare water. These diverting ditches are called spillways.

● **Dam it.** Dams are horribly handy for flood control. But are they any good? Who better to ask than a couple of horrible hydrologists? The only problem is finding two hydrologists that agree. About anything! Take these two, for a start:

DAMS ARE BRILLIANT BECAUSE THEY STOP RIVERS FLOODING, AND WE KNOW HOW USEFUL THAT IS. AND THEY MAKE SURE THERE'S A STEADY SUPPLY OF WATER FOR DRINKING AND FARMING. AND THEY CAN GENERATE LOADS OF CHEAP CLEAN ELECTRICITY. WHAT MORE COULD YOU ASK?

DAM BUILDER

DAMS ARE DISASTROUS BECAUSE THEY FORCE MILLIONS OF PEOPLE OUT OF THEIR HOUSES AND DROWN THE LAND UNDER TONNES OF WATER. THEY ALSO WIPE OUT WILDLIFE. AND IF YOU WAVE GOODBYE TO FLOODS, IT'S BYE BYE FERTILE FLOOD-PLAINS AND DELTAS TOO. BESIDES DAMS COST A FORTUNE TO BUILD AND WHAT HAPPENS IF ONE GOES AND BURSTS?

DAM BUSTER

Talk about putting a spanner in the works! It's difficult to know just who to believe.

• **Build an embankment**. One of the oldest ways to stop a flood is to make the riverbank higher. You could do this by building a mud or concrete embankment, or dyke. But does this waterproofing work? The answer is, Sometimes it does, and sometimes it doesn't. Along the Mississippi, embankments are called levees. (That's French for "raised".) There are thousands of kilometres of them along the river. For years, they've been the main flood-proofing measure. But what happens when a levee springs a leak? Then things go horribly wrong, as the terrible true story on the next page shows...

Raging river fact file

NAME: Mississippi River

LOCATION: USA

LENGTH: 3,780 km

SOURCE: Lake Itasca, Minnesota, USA

DRAINS: 3,256,000 sq km

MOUTH: Flows into the Gulf of Mexico (part of the Atlantic Ocean) at its huge delta.

FLOW FACTS:

• Its longest tributary, the Missouri, is actually 350 km longer than the Mississippi itself. The two rivers meet near St Louis.

• New Orleans is protected by several long levees. Which is just as well because the city lies below river level!

• Its nicknames include Old Man River and Big Muddy.

WHAT THEY SAID ABOUT IT: "You cannot tame that lawless stream." (Mark Twain)

After the Great Flood, summer 1993

For millions of people living along the Mississippi floods are a fact of life. But things seemed to be getting better. It had been 20 years since the last big flood and, with higher and stronger levees, backed up by new dams and spillways, floods seemed a thing of the past.

The new measures seemed to have done the trick. Or had they? True, it had been a very wet year with record-breaking rains. But the floods, if they came, usually happened in spring. By summer, the river was usually falling. What happened that summer took everyone by surprise.

With no break in the rain, the Mississippi became a raging torrent, flowing at six times its usual speed. In places, it rose seven metres above normal, a raging brown torrent of water and mud.

The new flood measures failed miserably. In the state of Illinois alone, 17 levees crumbled under the strain ... including the one protecting the little town of Valmeyer.

Local people worked round the clock, filling thousands of sandbags to fight back the flow. But despite their best efforts, they could not stop the wall of water which poured into the town.

Fortunately, the town had just been evacuated. Miraculously, only one person died and no one was seriously injured. Everyone knew that it could have been much worse.

Three weeks later, the townspeople were allowed to return home to start the massive clean-up. Valmeyer had been turned into a waterlogged ghost town. Windows were smashed, all the lights were out, and thick muddy sludge covered everything. The eerie quietness was broken only by the buzzing of huge swarms of mosquitoes.

"It's heartbreaking," one man said as he looked at the wreckage of his home. "I've lived here all my life and it's all gone. Everything's covered in mud and mould. But at least we've got each other and a disaster sure makes folk rally round." Only four houses were left standing. Others were water-filled wrecks. Their only occupants were frogs, crayfish and ... poisonous snakes. Everyone had to up sticks and start all over again. (And after a second soaking in September, that's exactly what happened. The whole town moved lock, stock and barrel, to higher, drier ground.)

The Great Flood of 1993 was America's worst natural disaster. The flood covered an area the size of England and seven states were declared disaster zones. The water caused $10 billion of damage, flooded 50 towns, destroyed 43,000 homes and left 70,000 people homeless. Millions of acres of crops were washed away. And only a quarter of the levees were left in one piece.

Earth-shattering fact
Imagine a busy city like London. Now imagine it under a metre of water... All it would take is a high tide surging up the River Thames from the sea. To stop such a disaster, a massive barrier was built across the Thames in 1984. When high tides are due, ten huge steel gates swing up from the river bed to make a gigantic dam. The barrier's already had to close more than 30 times...

Travis's top waterproof flood warnings

If building a dam is beyond you, or your homework doesn't leave you enough time, what on Earth can you do if a flood's flowing your way? Try to remember these basic Do's and Don'ts and you'll save yourself from a soaking:

DO…
* Stay tuned to your radio for flood warnings.

Or listen out for a siren, if time's short. Some countries run a telephone flood-warning service. If you can get to the phone…

* Switch off the gas and electricity. Water and electricity are an explosive mix. NEVER touch electrical equipment with wet hands. Ever. Water is a brilliant conductor of electricity which means that electricity can shoot through it very easily indeed. And it could give you a killer shock.

* Stock up on sandbags. If you're staying put, block up doorways and air bricks with sandbags. You can buy them or make your own from some strong cloth sacks and sand.

• Go upstairs. And take any other people, pets and valuables with you, out of reach of the water.

• Pack some supplies. Whether you're going or staying, you'll need emergency stores to tide you over for a few days. Pack warm clothes, blankets, food, water, a torch and some batteries. Stuff these in strong plastic bags ready to grab when you need them.

• Be prepared to leave home. If the flood's really serious, you may have to move fast. Head for higher ground away from the river. Better still, go to stay with some friends.

Once you're outside…

DON'T…

• Try to cross any floodwater by foot. If it reaches your ankles, turn back and find another route. The water may be deeper than it looks and the road underneath may have been washed away.

• Go for a drive. At least, not through flood water. It often flows fast enough to wash cars away. And cars can quickly turn into death-traps if you break down. By the time the water reaches the windows, the water pressure will be too strong for you to open the door. If you do have to drive, open the windows before you set off. That'll equalize the pressure inside and outside the car.

• Drink any floodwater. However thirsty you are. Floodwater's filthy, thanks to all the mud, debris and even sewage it sucks along. Ideal for germs to fester in. If you're staying at home, fill the bath with clean water, and boil any water you use.

• Camp near a river bed. Even if it looks dry. It could fill up in seconds and wash you away.

• Ever try to outrun the flood. However fast you run, it'll be right behind you.

You might think that spending your whole life studying water might turn a hydrologist's brain horribly soggy and soft. But these soaking scientists are not as wet as they seem.

They're working their socks off trying to forecast floods more accurately. The good news is that they're getting quicker at spotting the warning signs and moving people out of the way. The bad news is that forecasts can never be watertight. It can't be a cut and dried case. Why? Well, floods are just too horribly unpredictable.

REVOLTING RIVERS

Never mind messing about on rivers. After everything rivers have done for us, what are we doing in return? The sickening answer is making a mess of them. Horrible humans have made some rivers so disgustingly dirty, they've been declared officially DEAD! (The revolting rivers, not the humans. Though if your drinking water came from one of them, you might soon be a gonner too.) So why on Earth is freshwater so filthy? Why not...

Make you own rancid river soup

What you need:

- stinking sewage (it's usually treated in a sewage works before it's clean enough to be pumped into the river but in some places it goes in ... as it is!)
- filthy factory waste (this might be dirty water or poisonous metals and chemicals)
- fertilizers and pesticides (washed off farmers' fields)

What you do:

1 Chuck all the ingredients into a river and leave to fester.

2 Sprinkle a few bottles and tin cans on top.

3 Now offer a bowlful to your teacher!

154

HORRIBLE HEALTH WARNING

Slurping even one spoonful of rancid river soup could seriously damage your teacher's health. We take clean water for granted but river water can be full of all kinds of nasty germs – especially with humans pumping all kinds of waste and sewage into rivers. And it's not just humans who are at risk. River pollution kills hundreds of plants and animals. Take the very rare Yangtze River dolphin. Pollution's pushed it to the brink of extinction. But it's not the only problem. Dolphins use hearing to find their way. But there's so much traffic on the river that it's too noisy for the dolphins to navigate and many of them die in accidental collisions with boats.

Raging river fact file

NAME: River Ganges

LOCATION: India and Bangladesh

LENGTH: 2,510 km

SOURCE: Gangotri glacier, Himalayas

MOUTH: Flows into the Indian Ocean at the Bay of Bengal.

DRAINS: 975,900 sq km

FLOW FACTS:

● It joins the Brahmaputra River in Bangladesh and empties into the world's biggest delta.

● A huge mangrove swamp stretches along the delta. It's home to man-eating crocodiles and tigers.

● About half a billion people live on its floodplain.

Cleaning up the gungy Ganges

For millions of people living along the Ganges, the river doubles up as a water supply and a drain. They don't have the money for posh treatment plants, so every day, millions of litres of smelly sewage and killer chemicals are flushed straight into the river. And that's not all...

Many people believe that the river is holy and that bathing in its water will wash their sins away. People also come to the river to die. Their bodies are cremated (burnt), then their ashes are thrown into the water. Sometimes bodies are also thrown in. Animal and human bodies. It may sound morbid to you but for people in India it's very important. The problem is that it's not doing the river much good. Some of the Ganges is so horribly polluted that it's putting people's health at risk.

In 1985 things got so bad that a massive clean-up campaign began. Part of the plan was to build hundreds of new sewage treatment works. (Warning – you'll need a strong stomach for the next bit.) Another part of the plan was to flood the river with turtles. Yes, turtles. Meat-eating turtles who would munch up the dead. Gruesome but brilliant.

But has it worked? Is the gungy Ganges now gleaming with health? Well, not exactly; but it's certainly getting cleaner – though how much of that is down to the tasteless turtles, no one can really tell.

Earth-shattering fact

In 1858, the smell from the River Thames was so bad that it put MPs (Members of Parliament) in the nearby Houses of Parliament right off their work. They renamed the river the Great Stink. Thank goodness things have got a bit more fragrant.

Fragrant flowers

But it isn't all doom and gloom. The good news is that people are really trying to clean up their act. On many rivers, action plans are already up and running. Remember the reeking Rhine? For years it was known as the 'sewer of Europe'. Well, things are now looking up. The river was well-stocked with salmon until about 50 years ago. (Salmon are particularly sensitive to pollution.) The aim is to bring the salmon swimming back in the next few years. And there are strict rules to help it happen.

Which is great news for raging rivers all over the world. And for you. Before very long, you'll be back by the riverbank, a drink and a fishing rod in your hands, with not a horrible field trip in sight...

ODIOUS OCEANS

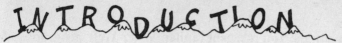 INTRODUCTION

Geography. It's a horrible word, isn't it? And what on Earth does it mean? Is it all about boring old rivers in boring old valleys in boring old countries you can't even spell? The answer is yes, it's all these things, but it's a whole lot more besides. Don't let your teacher go into details. The horrible truth about geography teachers is that they never know when to stop.

So what do geographers actually do? Try this experiment. Stare out of the window and have a good look outside. Look harder. What can you see? A clump of trees? Some clouds in the sky? A rolling field? The road into town? (The dog digging up your mum's prize dahlias?)

* That's the posh name for a huge wave which rushes up a river from the sea with the incoming tide. And NOTHING TO DO WITH TEACHERS!

163

Congratulations! You're a geographer. Why? Well, geography is actually made up of two old Greek words which mean "the science of describing the world". And that's what you've been doing. (The dog won't get off so lightly!)

But geography can also be horribly misleading. Take calling our planet "Earth", for example. Not a very clever way to describe a place that's covered in far more water than land. Far better to call it planet "Ocean". The oceans are the biggest places on the planet by far. And the awesome odious oceans are what this book is all about.

In *Odious Oceans*, you can...

• dive down to the deepest depths with Dirk, the deep-sea diver.

(* Posh term for a geographer who studies the sea.)

• learn to love a great white shark (you can do it!).

- find out why the *Titanic* really sank.
- see if you've got what it takes to join up with the Navy.

You'll never think geography's boring again.

GOING DOWN

A journey to the bottom of the sea (almost)

On the morning of 23 January 1960, at 8.15 a.m. on the dot, two men smiled nervously, said goodbye to their shipmates and entered a tiny steel capsule hanging beneath a huge, cigar-shaped tank.

They were about to embark on the voyage of their lives, and earn a place in the geography books. The capsule was only the size of a small car, and packed with so much equipment that there was barely space for the men to sit down. But then no one had said it was going to be a comfortable ride. Slowly, the ship's crane heaved and groaned into action and lowered the capsule overboard, into the dark waters of the Pacific Ocean. The two men shook hands and wished each other luck. Their descent into the unknown had begun...

The two men were scientists, Dr Jacques Piccard and Lieutenant Don Walsh of the US Navy. Their extraordinary craft was called *Trieste*. Technically, it was known as a bathyscaphe (bath-ee-scafe), like a mini-submarine. The scientists' mission was to dive to the bottom of the Challenger Deep, in the monstrous Marianas Trench, a gigantic gash in the seabed, and the deepest spot known on the planet. *No one had ever tried this before. No one even knew if you could.*

Piccard and Walsh sat anxiously in cramped silence as *Trieste* sank down through the dark icy waters, waiting for their echo-sounder to warn them that they were nearing the bottom.

They knew only too well how fraught with danger their journey was. But neither knew what lay beneath them. Or if *Trieste* would stand the strain. And that wasn't all. All that separated them from the crushing weight or pressure of the water above them (imagine having a lorry balanced on your thumbnail) was the capsule's thick, steel walls. At about 9,000 metres, they put on the brakes to slow *Trieste*'s descent – a crash landing would be disastrous. Suddenly, there was a sickening CRAACKK!

"What on earth was that?" said Piccard, looking round nervously.

For a moment, their hearts were in their mouths ... but it was a false alarm. One of *Trieste*'s outer windows had cracked under the tremendous weight of the water. But the capsule itself stayed watertight. The men breathed a huge sigh of relief. Then came the moment they had been waiting for … and dreading. At 1.06 p.m., a nail-biting four hours and 48 minutes after leaving the surface, *Trieste* bumped and grated along the silty bottom of the Challenger Deep and came to a juddering halt.

Hearts thumping, Piccard and Walsh switched on their floodlights, and peered into a world no one had ever seen before – the deepest, darkest depths of the oceans. And from somewhere in that eerie darkness, something was staring back. But that was impossible – nothing could live this far down! There wasn't enough oxygen in the water for anything to survive. Surely? Not for the first time, or for the last, science was to be proved wrong. The staring something was a ghostly white flat fish a bit like a flounder. And it was very much alive. Soon afterwards, a small, reddish creature, shaped like a shrimp, also went scuttling past.

Teeth chattering with cold, Piccard and Walsh spent 20 minutes on the seabed, munching on chocolate bars for nourishment. Then, releasing two tonnes of iron-pellet ballast which had kept *Trieste* weighted down, they began their slow, steady ascent, breaking the surface at 4.56 p.m., three hours and 17 minutes later.

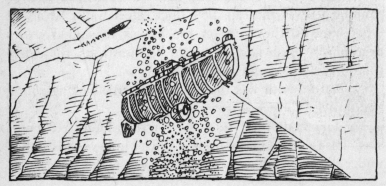

Their journey of 22 kilometres had taken eight and a half hours. They had dived to a depth of almost 11 kilometres, deeper than anyone else ... before or since. Piccard and Walsh's amazing record still stands today, as the deepest dive ever made. And one of the greatest feats of ocean exploration ever.

THE ODIOUS OCEANS

While exploring the odious oceans in a mini-sub might be way out of your depth, there are plenty of much safer ways of getting to know them better. But, wait a minute, don't plunge in just yet, there are a couple of things you'll need to know about oceans first. For example:

- where on Earth are they?
- what on Earth are they?
- why on Earth are they there in the first place? (OK, so that's three things, but who's counting?)

Look at the map opposite for starters.

As you can see, oceans are absolutely HUGE. They're also hugely wet and salty. And full of extraordinary plants and animals. Actually, the oceans are so odiously vast, that there are still hundreds of kilometres of silty seabed which no one has ever seen ... yet. In fact, until recently, geographers thought that most of the seabed was just boringly sandy and flat. (Of course, none of them had been there, so none of them really knew. And they had to say something.) Now we know that there are high mountains, plunging valleys, active volcanoes, rumbling earthquakes, rolling plains – you get the picture – all covered up by the water. Awesome.

Fascinating facts about the odious oceans

1 The odious oceans cover two-thirds of the Earth. Like we said before, they're big! And over half of this water is in just one ocean – the Pacific. Next in order of size come the Atlantic, Indian, Southern and Arctic oceans. For most of the year, the f-f-freezing Arctic Ocean is covered in a thick sheet of ice with the North Pole stuck in the middle. The Southern Ocean is icy too but that's the least of its problems. Some horrible geographers say it doesn't exist! They claim

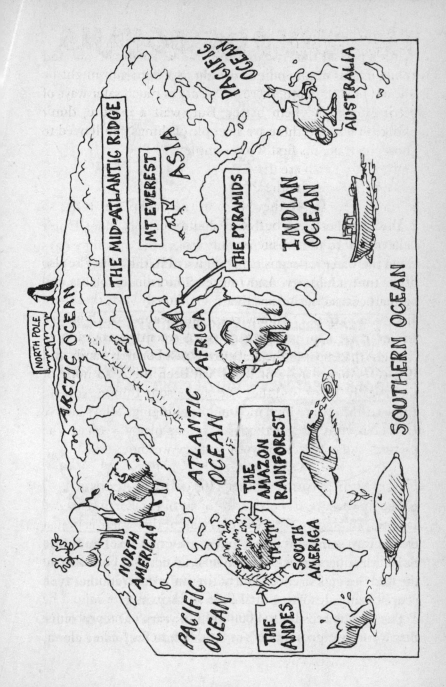

that it's part of the Atlantic, Indian and Pacific oceans and not an odious ocean in its own right. Spoilsports.

2 Your teachers may tell you that the sea is blue. Don't believe a word of it. The sea only looks blue on sunny days when the water reflects blue light rays from the sun. The rest of the time it looks greenish or grey. The greener the sea, the better, because this means that...

By the way, some seas aren't green, grey, or blue. The White Sea is white because it's covered in ice. And, very occasionally the Red Sea gets so chock-full of tiny red plants (another type of appetizing algae) that it takes on a pinky tinge.

3 The oceans are about 4,000 million years old (even older than your grandparents). Not long before they came along, the Earth formed from a cloud of dust and gas. As it cooled and solidified, water vapour (that's water in gas form) rose into the air from violent volcanoes on the surface. The vapour cooled and formed storm clouds, and torrential rain poured and filled the first oceans with water.

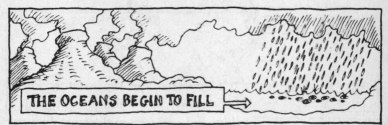

THE OCEANS BEGIN TO FILL

4 The very first oceans weren't great places for holidays. Forget warm, salty water and long, sandy beaches. The water was boiling hot, with a bitter taste like vinegar. Today it's salty because, well, it's got salt in it. Just like the stuff you put on your chips.

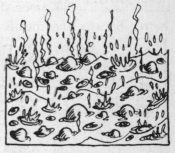

Some of this comes from undersea volcanoes. Some falls in the rain. Most comes from rocks on land, washed into the sea by rivers. And there's plenty of it. Enough, in fact, to cover the Earth with a layer 150 metres thick.

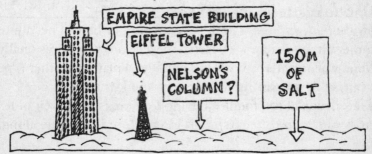

EMPIRE STATE BUILDING
EIFFEL TOWER
NELSON'S COLUMN?
150M OF SALT

5 The geographical name for common old saltiness is salinity. To be horribly technical, it's measured as the number of parts of salt in one thousand parts of water. This is measured as p.s.u. (practical salinity units). The more salt in the sea, the better you float.

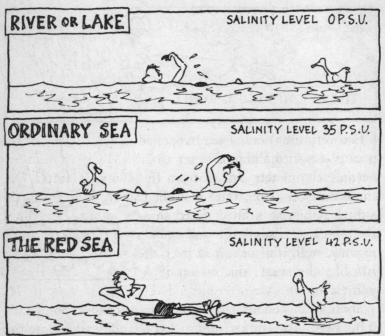

RIVER OR LAKE   SALINITY LEVEL O P.S.U.

ORDINARY SEA   SALINITY LEVEL 35 P.S.U.

THE RED SEA   SALINITY LEVEL 42 P.S.U.

Try this simple taste test.

How to rustle up the Red Sea
You will need:
some salt
some warm water
a bucket or measuring jug
a few drops of red food colouring (optional)

What to do:

1 Put four level teaspoons of salt into a litre of water.

2 Stir until all the salt dissolves.

3 Add a few drops of red food colouring. (This *is* the Red Sea, remember.)

4 Take a sip (just a small one).

That's how salty the Red Sea is!

6 Some funny things have happened in the history of the oceans. About 6.5 million years ago, the Mediterranean Sea became completely cut off from the odious Atlantic. One thousand years later, the sea water had all dried up in the sun, leaving the seabed caked in salt a kilometre thick. Eventually the sea level rose again in the Atlantic and a gigantic waterfall splashed over the Straits of Gibraltar (that's the channel that joins the Atlantic and Med) and poured into the Mediterranean. Even so it took roughly 100 years for the Mediterranean to fill up again.

7 It's a bit misleading to call the sea "level". Like everything else, it has its ups and downs. During the last Ice Age, 18,000 years ago, so much water was locked up in glaciers, that the sea level dropped by 100 metres. Enough to make it possible to walk from England to France – if you'd got a couple of days to spare. Since then, it's risen about 10 cm every 100 years. Geographers know how sea levels have risen in the last 5,000 years because they've found the bones and teeth of land-living mammals, like mammoths and horses, in the seabed. They all drowned when the sea level rose.

CHANGES IN WORLD-WIDE SEA LEVELS ARE CALLED 'EUSTATIC' CHANGES, I'M NOT TOO ECSTATIC ABOUT THEM MY SELF!

FRANCE

Teacher teaser

Just how in-depth is your teacher's geography? Scratch your head as if you're deep in thought and ask:

PLEASE, SIR, HOW HEAVY IS THE SEA?

Answer: The water in the sea weighs an incredible 1.2 QUINTILLION tonnes! That's 1,200,000,000,000,000,000 tonnes. And that's just for starters. The deeper you go, the heavier it feels. This is called water pressure. In the deepest ocean, the water pressure is like having 20 elephants sitting on top of you. Ouch!

Earth-shattering fact
Once upon a time, people believed that the Earth was flat. They thought that if you sailed too far in one direction, you'd fall off the edge and end up in Hell! An even more Earth-shattering fact is that some people still think this.

Some salty seas

Did you know that some parts of the oceans aren't called oceans at all? They're seas. To make matters worse, some seas aren't really seas, but salty lakes. As a rule, a real sea is a part of an ocean. So the South China Sea is part of the Pacific Ocean and the North Sea is part of the Atlantic Ocean. Confused? Try dipping your toes into these salty seas:

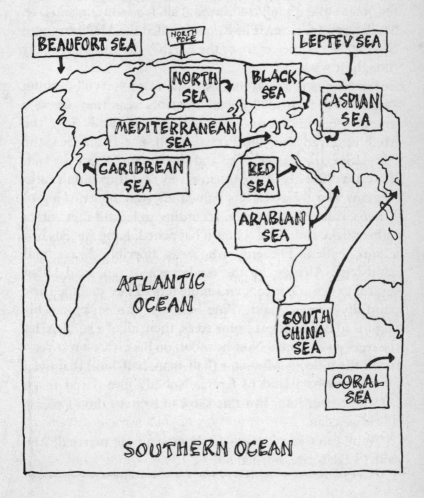

Black Sea The ancient Greeks called this "the hospitable sea", even though it was horribly rocky and stormy. They thought that it was unlucky to give a thing a bad name, however nasty it actually turned out to be. Later the Turks changed the sea's name because it scared them to death!

Dead Sea This sea is called "dead" because its water's so salty nothing can live in it for long. It's five times saltier than most of the oceans. But it's not really a sea at all. It's a salty, inland lake.

Mediterranean Sea The Romans called the Mediterranean Sea the "sea at the centre of the Earth". Because they really thought it was.

Seven Seas Ancient sailors used the word "seven" to mean "many". And "many" meant the only seas they knew, a grand total of seven. These were the Red Sea, the Mediterranean Sea, the Persian Gulf, the Black Sea, the China Sea, the Caspian Sea and the Indian Ocean. In fact, there are more like 70 seas than seven. But they didn't care.

Aegean Sea This sea was named after an ancient king of Athens, called Aegeus, who according to legend met with a rather sticky end. This is how it happened. King Aegeus had a son, called Theseus, who was horribly brave and handsome. Already, by the tender age of ten, he'd killed several gruesome giants and monsters. They included the painfully-named giant, Pine-bender, who strapped his victims to two bent-over pine trees, then, all of a sudden, let the trees go ... Ouch! Now he set off on his greatest test yet – to kill the hideous Minotaur (half-man, half-bull) that lived on the nearby island of Crete. Nobody else dared to go anywhere near him. But this show of bravery didn't please Theseus's dad.

"Why can't you just stay at home and get married?" he said. "Like a nice, normal boy."

178

"No way," replied Theseus. (He could be stubborn, too.)

"Oh all right," Aegeus sighed. "You win. But if you do kill the Minotaur, instead of the other way round, please, please, please change your sails from black to white as you sail home. Then I'll know you're safe."

"No problem, Dad," said Theseus, not really listening. "See you later."

To cut a long story short, Theseus reached Crete, and proved himself brave enough to kill the Minotaur and handsome enough to get himself engaged to Ariadne, daughter of the King of Crete. She'd fancied him for ages and ages. She sailed home with Theseus to meet his mum and dad. On the way back, the two love-birds stopped at the island of Naxos for the night. But while Ariadne was fast asleep, Theseus sailed off and left her. Just like that. No note, no nothing.

When Ariadne woke up and found herself abandoned, she was FURIOUS.

Luckily, she had friends in high places, including a god, called Dionysus. (He fancied Ariadne.) He played a trick on Theseus and made him forget his promise. You remember, the one about changing his sails? So, Theseus sailed off home, without a care, black sails a-blazing. What a mistake! Thinking him dead, poor old Aegeus went mad with grief, leapt off a cliff into the sea and was drowned. So Athens lost a king but gained a name for a sea.

THE DAILY GLOBE
GHASTLY GOINGS-ON DOWN UNDER

What is the deep seabed really like? Is it really deeply dull, boring and flat? Or are the rumours of mountains, volcanoes and valleys actually true? Is the deep sea floor all it's cracked up to be? We at *The Daily Globe* were determined to get to the bottom of things. So we sent our roving reporter, C. Shanty, on a special, record-breaking assignment...

Underwater mountain bigger than Everest shock!

It's official! Everest is not the highest mountain on Earth. At a paltry 8,848 metres, Everest is over ONE KILOMETRE (that's 1,000 metres) shorter than majestic Mauna Kea.

MAUNA KEA

EVEREST

This gigantic volcano in the Pacific Ocean rises an astonishing 10,203 metres from the sea floor. And that's a world record. The tip of the mountain breaks the surface of the sea and sprouts into a heavenly Hawaiian island. As you can see, while I was there, I took some time off to explore...

Spreading ridges – is the Atlantic cracking up?

Back on the job, I set sail for the middle of the Atlantic Ocean. Under this ocean, so I'm told, runs the world's longest mountain chain. Straight down the middle, all the way from Iceland (where you can see it sticking out of the sea) to Antarctica lies the boringly named Mid-Atlantic Ridge. It's over 11,000 km long, with mountains 4 km tall. In most places it lies a whopping 2 km underwater.

WET BIT

DRY BIT

MID-ATLANTIC RIDGE

OVER 11,000 KM LONG AND 4 KM HIGH

To tell you the truth, it's not as boring as it sounds. All along the ridge, red-hot, runny rock seeps up through cracks in the seabed. As it hits the water, cools and goes solid, it builds up brand-new mountains and volcanoes.

And, clever old ridge, it also makes new seabed. At the last count, the Atlantic was getting wider each year, by a whole 4 cm! Geographers call this "seafloor spreading". Because, er, it's the seafloor and, well, it's spreading … but I didn't have time to wait around to watch.

Hitting the depths in the murky Marianas

Next, to the north-west Pacific and the murky Marianas Trench. This place holds the record for the deepest, darkest place on Earth. And the spookiest, take it from me.

But it's not the only trench in the sea. A trench is a huge, ghastly gash in the sea floor, which happens when one piece of seabed is pushed under another and melts back into the Earth. This is called subduction, a posh way of saying pushing under. And it's just as well it happens. Trenches balance out seafloor spreading and stop the Earth getting bigger and bigger. Imagine the chaos that would cause! I'd never get back to the office. Come to think of it…

The Marianas Trench is a staggering 11,034 m deep.

Lose your flipper down there, and it'll take ONE WHOLE HOUR to reach the bottom! Luckily, I kept my flippers firmly on my feet.

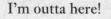

Top secret – dead bodies litter ocean floor

They cover over half the sea floor, stretching for kilometres on end. They're flatter than anywhere on land. They're the truly abysmal abyssal plains. But it's not their flatness that makes the hairs on your neck stand on end. These awful places are covered in a ghastly carpet of ooze, made from the bodies of billions and billions of miniscule sea creatures which have rained down from the surface. Billions of DEAD sea creatures.

I'm outta here!

Who boasts the most coast?

Back on land (phew!), the coastlines can break a few records too. Did you know that if all the world's coastlines were straightened out, they'd stretch round the Earth 13 times? Congratulations, Canada! Not only are you one of the world's largest countries but with over 90,000 km of seashore, you can also boast the most coast. In second place is Indonesia, with a paltry 47,000 km.

CANADA: SOME GREAT WIGGLY BITS

And finally, you will need to fly south to the north coast of Hawaii to find the world's highest sea cliffs. Dive over the edge and you've a whole kilometre to fall before you finally reach the sea. You wouldn't catch me getting too close to the edge. Which is precisely why I'm finishing this report from the safety of the lounge in the Ocean View Hotel. Cheers!

CHEERS!

A moving story

Ever fancied a house by the sea? Sounds great, doesn't it, but in fact it can be horribly tough living along the coast, what with the wind, waves and weather constantly pounding against the shore and eating away at the rocks and cliffs. This is called erosion, and it doesn't half grind you down. The way waves crash into the shore is called "breaking". Here's what happens:

How to ride a breaking wave
What you will need:
a seashore
a surfboard
a willing victim (actually, the willing bit's not essential)

What to do:
We've asked Dirk the deep-sea diver to show you the ropes:
1 The wave starts off smooth and low. So far, so good.

2 As it nears the shore, it slows down because of friction* with the sea floor.**

(*Friction is a force which tries to stop things moving past each other. Try sliding your fingertips along your desk. Friction makes them harder and harder to move.)
(**Oceanographers call this "feeling the bottom". But that's quite enough of that. Snigger.)

3 It gets steeper and taller…

4 …until it topples over and breaks on the shore. Aaaaghh!

Making waves

Because of waves and currents, the odious oceans are constantly on the move. But what on Earth are they? Waves are made by the wind blowing across the surface of the sea. The stronger the wind, the bigger the waves. And some can be horribly huge. In 1933, the unfortunate crew of a ship called USS *Ramapo* had the fright of their lives when a wave, measuring 34 metres high (that's higher than a ten-storey building), reared its ugly head in front of them. Luckily, they lived to tell the tale.

THEY HAD GOOD REASON TO BE RATTLED. WAVES ARE INCREDIBLY STRONG. IN 1968 A GIGANTIC WAVE HIT AN OIL TANKER OFF THE COAST OF AFRICA, AND SNAPPED THE SHIP CLEAN IN TWO!

If you want to go out in rough weather, it's probably safest to travel by submarine. Waves only ruffle the surface of the water, so if you're deep enough down, you won't feel a thing.

Try making some waves of your own. They'll be a bit smaller than the real thing, of course. Fill a bowl with water and blow across the surface. Remember, the harder you blow, the bigger the waves. Go on, blow harder! If your mum tells you off for making a mess, look shocked and say:

BUT MUM, I WAS JUST STUDYING SIMPLE OSCILLATIONS!

THAT'S "WAVES" TO YOU AND ME

Troublesome tidal waves

Tidal waves are:

a) not really waves at all (because they aren't caused by the wind) and

b) nothing to do with tides.

They're triggered off by earthquakes or volcanoes deep beneath the sea. These send shock waves quivering through the water which make it bulge and ripple. At first, the ripples aren't much to look at – in fact, they can pass ships by without anyone noticing. But they're speedy movers, racing along as fast as jet planes, until they reach the land. Then the trouble really starts. They rear up over 30 metres high, and crash down again with a mighty SPLASH!

One type of tidal wave contains enough water to drown a whole island. Geographers call these waves tsunamis (soo-naa-mees), a Japanese word meaning "harbour waves". The largest ever was 85 metres high. In 1946, a tsunami in Hawaii picked up a house, carried it a few hundred metres down the road and put it down again. So gently that the breakfast plates were still on the table!

Undercover currents

Swirling about just under the surface are huge rivers of water called currents. These are swept along by the wind. But what on Earth do they do? Some currents are warm (up to a sizzling 30°C); others are cold (down to a chilly -2°C). They take warm water from near the equator and cold water from near the poles, and carry it around the world. This helps to heat up and cool down the land more evenly. Without crucial currents, the equator would get hotter, and the poles would get colder. And that would make life very uncomfortable. Some currents are huge. One current, the chilly West Wind Drift, flows around Antarctica, carrying 2,000 times more water than the mighty Amazon River in Brazil, the largest river in the world!

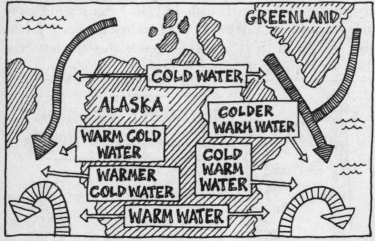

Tricky tides

It's not just waves or currents that keep the oceans in non-stop motion. Twice a day, the sea rises and floods on to the seashore. And twice a day, it flows out again. The posh word for this is "ebbing". These changes are called the tides.

High tide is when the water is in. Low tide's when it's out again. Tides are mainly caused by the moon's gravity pulling the oceans nearest to it into a giant bulge. But that's not all. While all this is going on, the Earth is spinning on its axis (an imaginary line running down its middle). And as it spins, it pulls the oceans on the other side into another bulge. Confused? Don't be. See Dirk's deep-sea diagram No. 1.

Dirk's deep-sea diagram No. 1

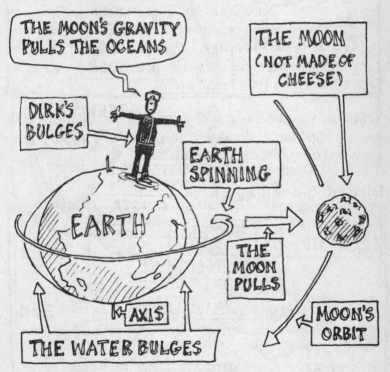

To muddle matters more, twice a month the sun gets in on the action. When the sun and moon pull in a straight line, they cause very high high-waters and very low low-waters.

These are called spring tides. See deep-sea diagram No. 2.

Dirk's deep-sea diagram No. 2

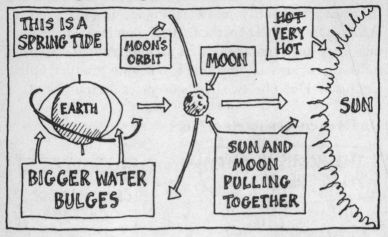

When the sun and moon pull at right angles, there are high low tides and low high tides. If you see what I mean. These are called neap tides. See diagram No. 3.

Dirk's deep-sea diagram No. 3

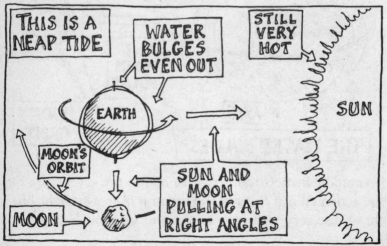

Dirk's deep-sea diagram No. 4

The Bermuda Triangle *or* There are three parts to every story

One particularly perilous part of the oceans is the baffling Bermuda Triangle. It's a huge, triangular stretch of the Atlantic Ocean, between Puerto Rico, Miami and Bermuda. And it's been puzzling geographers for years. Why? Well, in the last 40 years, the troublesome Triangle has swallowed up at least 100 ships and hundreds of unfortunate sailors. Never to be seen again.

For example, in 1918, a huge great coal ship, called *Cyclops* vanished without trace while crossing the Triangle, with all

309 of its crew. But the trouble started long before that. In 1881, one ship, carrying a cargo of timber, lost three crews in a week, before disappearing altogether! In most cases, ships disappear in calm weather, for no apparent reason. And they vanish so fast that they don't have time to send out an SOS.

And it's not just ships. Picture the scene. It's 5 December 1944. The Second World War is raging. Five US Navy torpedo bombers, each with a three-man crew, are flying over the sea en route from Florida. One by one, as they cross the Triangle, they vanish into thin air... The day is clear and sunny. Their instruments are working perfectly. A rescue plane is dispatched to find them. Within minutes, it too has disappeared!

What on Earth is going on? Is it coincidence, or something more sinister? Who or what is to blame? Here are some possible culprits:

1 The weather in this part of the Atlantic can be awfully unpredictable. You can have blue skies one minute and a howling gale the next. The worst sorts of storm are hurricanes. These tropical terrors can blow ships off course or smash them to smithereens.

2 Ships might also be sunk by waterspouts. These are swirling funnels of air. They hang down from storm clouds over the sea. When the swirling air touches down on the water, the water is sucked up by the air to make a huge column of spray. These columns can be over a kilometre tall. But waterspouts only hang about for 10–15 minutes. After that you'd need to DUCK!, as all that water comes crashing back down.

3 What about massive underwater explosions? Could they hold the key? In 1995, scientists discovered a huge build-up of methane gas under the seabed. One scientist said:

RELEASING THIS GAS WOULD BE LIKE SHAKING AN ENORMOUS CAN OF POP. THE OCEAN WOULD FIZZ UP AND SHIPS LOSE ALL BUOYANCY AND SINK WITHOUT A TRACE IN MINUTES. WATER CONTAINING HUGE AMOUNTS OF GAS IS LESS DENSE THAN NORMAL, SO BOATS WOULD SINK AND PLANES PLUMMET.

(PS There'd also be a terrible pong – methane smells awful!)

4 Metal that's formed underneath the ocean floor could act like a massive magnet. Something certainly confuses ships' compasses in the triangle. And this might cause them to sail in the wrong direction and get hopelessly lost!

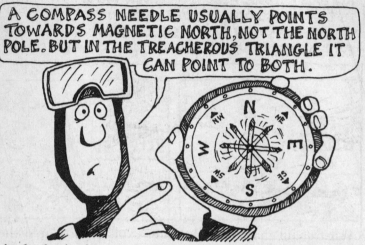

A COMPASS NEEDLE USUALLY POINTS TOWARDS MAGNETIC NORTH, NOT THE NORTH POLE. BUT IN THE TREACHEROUS TRIANGLE IT CAN POINT TO BOTH.

5 And why is the wreckage never found? Well, that might have something to do with odious ocean currents. The surging Gulf Stream can carry debris far away before the search team can find it. Small whirlpools, called eddies, help to scatter the wreckage.

6 Once under water, debris is also quickly buried by sand or silt on the sea floor. On the other hand, it could be sucked into a "blue hole", whatever that is!

ACTUALLY, A BLUE HOLE IS AN UNDER-WATER CAVE IN THE SIDE OF AN ISLAND, CURRENTS FLOWING THROUGH THESE HOLES CAN EASILY SUCK A SMALL BOAT DOWN, ER... AS I'M ABOUT TO FIND OUT!

As for lost crews, their bodies are quite probably gobbled up by sharks.

What do you think? At least these theories sound as if they could be true. Which is more than can be said for others. Some people claim that ships entering the Triangle are snatched by aliens in flying saucers who use the sailors in extraterrestrial experiments. Weird.

If all this mystery has made you peckish (it affects some people like that), don't worry. You won't have to wait very long for a snack. The next chapter is crammed full of mouth-watering morsels. If they don't eat you first…

PLENTY MORE FISH IN THE SEA

For almost as long as they've lived on Earth, people have gone fishing. And in some places, methods haven't changed all that much. Fishermen still use the same trusty old spears, hooks and lines that they've been using for thousands of years. In Papua New Guinea (a country north-east of Australia), fishermen even use giant spiders' webs as nets (though they take the giant spiders out first).

Elsewhere in the world, fishing is big business – around 75 million tonnes of fish are caught every year. (That's a mind-boggling number of fish fingers!) Modern fishing trawlers are horribly high-tech. They find their fish using computers and sonar* and catch them in unbelievably big nets many kilometres long. Some ships are more like floating fish factories. They can clean, pack and freeze the fish while on board. That's bad luck if you happen to be a sardine. You're the fish they catch most of.

* SONAR IS AN INSTRUMENT WHICH SENDS OUT BEEPS OF SOUND. THESE HIT OBJECTS, SUCH AS SARDINES, AND SEND BACK ECHOES. THE ECHOES ARE PICKED UP BY ON-BOARD COMPUTERS AND SHOWN ON A SCREEN, THAT'S HOW YOU TELL WHERE THE FISH ARE.

BEEP!

BEEP!

FISH

What on Earth are fish?

Of course, you know what fish are but do you know what fish have in common? Any idea which two of these fishy facts are false?

1 Fish are cold-blooded. (Cold-blooded means they have to rely on outside conditions, like water temperature, to warm them up or cool them down.)

2 Fish live in salty and fresh water.

3 Fish breathe oxygen dissolved in the water.

4 Fish breathe through lungs, like humans.

5 Most fish are covered in scales.

6 Fish use their fins for steering and paddling.

7 All fish have bony skeletons.

8 Some fish can live out of water.

Answers: **4** and **7** are false.

4 Fish don't have lungs. Instead they breathe through slitty gills on the sides of their heads. As a fish swims along, it closes its gill covers, opens its mouth and gulps in water. Then it closes its mouth, opens its gills and forces the water out over them. This is when dissolved oxygen from the water goes into the fish's blood.

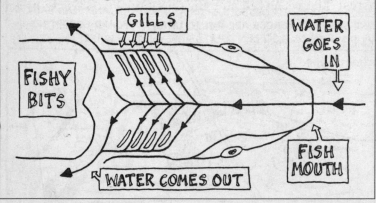

7 Sharks and rays have skeletons made of rubbery cartilage instead of bone. Press the end of your nose with your finger, go on, don't be shy! That's what cartilage feels like.

(By the way number 8 is true, believe it or not. Mudskippers are happy to be fish out of water but they need to keep their skin damp for taking in oxygen. They live at the muddy mouths of some rivers where the river meets the sea.)

Some very fishy record breakers

First The first fish appeared over 500 million years ago. They were just 4 centimetres long...

THAT'S THIS BIG!

with tiny teeth. Today, there are 25,000 fascinating fish species. And another hundred are discovered each year. In fact, there are as many different types of fish in the sea as there are amphibians, reptiles, birds and mammals put together. So there!

Fastest There's no catching the sensationally speedy sailfish. Over short distances, it's unbeatable. It races along at over 100 km/h, tucking its fins into its sides, to make it more aerodynamic.

ZOOM!

Slowest Seahorses are not only the oddest-looking fish in the oceans (how on Earth did they get those horse-shaped heads?), they're also the slowest swimmers. A seahorse in a tearing hurry takes three whole days to travel one kilometre! Stranger still, it's dad who has the babies. He grows a small pouch on his belly, into which the female squirts her eggs. (Then she swims off and leaves him to it.) Two weeks later, hundreds of baby seahorses shoot out. The first thing they do is learn to swim upright!

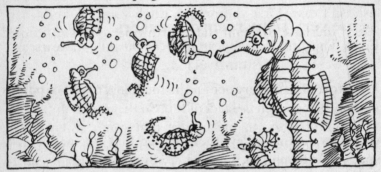

Best fliers To avoid being snapped up by hungry enemies, flying fish shoot out of the sea and glide through the air on wing-like fins. Like tiny fishy aeroplanes. Sometimes their enemies try to follow. A ship's cat was once lost overboard in the Atlantic Ocean, trying to grab a flying fish.

Smallest The titchiest fish in the big blue sea is the tiny dwarf goby from the Indian Ocean. It's so incredibly small it could swim up and down a tablespoon, with plenty of space to spare.

Oldest The longest-lived fish is thought to be an 88-year-old eel, called Putte, who died in 1948. She was born in the Sargasso Sea (part of the Atlantic Ocean) in 1860 but spent most of her life in a Swedish aquarium. Telling the age of a fish isn't easy. First you have to catch your fish and kill it. Then you have to count the growth rings on its scales and bones. Messy!

Greatest size difference In the tough old world of odious oceans, being eaten is a fact of life. So the ocean sunfish lays millions of eggs, to make sure that some survive. The newborn sunfish are the size of peas. But not for long. By the time they're adults, they're over a thousand times bigger – as big and heavy as small trucks. Awesome.

Riskiest to eat If you really want to dice with danger, try a portion of death pufferfish, the deadliest fish in the sea. Despite this, it's eaten as a delicacy in Japan where they call it fugu. Its heart, liver, blood and guts are so horribly poisonous, even the tiniest taste can kill you. Chefs are specially trained to take these bits out. But what if they get it wrong? One slight mistake and you're history.

First, you'll feel numb all over, then the shakes begin. A cure? Well, there isn't one really, though burying yourself up to your neck in mud is said to help a bit!

Greediest Fish get seasick – it's true! Especially if you shake them about in a bucket! (Don't try this at home!) Or if they eat themselves into a stupor. They don't come much greedier than the bad-mannered bluefish. It eats and eats until it makes itself sick. And then it starts eating all over again! Disgusting.

Largest catch In 1986, a Norwegian fishing boat caught 120 million fish – in one go. That's 30 fish for every Norwegian. The biggest fish ever caught with a rod was a whopping great white shark. It weighed more than a tonne.

And there's plenty more than just fish in the sea...

What on Earth are crabby crustaceans?

Strictly speaking, crustaceans aren't really fish. They're creatures like shrimps, crabs and lobsters. Most of them have hard shells to protect their soft bodies. And most live in water, except for woodlice – you might find one of these under a stone in your garden.

The biggest crustaceans are Japanese spider crabs. They're so huge, you could fit a horse between their huge front claws. They're also called "stilt-crabs" because their legs are so long. The biggest on record had a 3.6-metre legspan, and weighed a massive 18 kilograms. These colossal crustaceans live on the seabed. They eat other crustaceans, worms and molluscs. They won't go for you, though, unless your toes get too close for comfort.

Talking of your toes, you should watch out for the boxer crab. It has one of the nastiest nips. It cheats, though, by holding a stinging sea anemone in each of its pincers. Then, if an enemy gets too close, this crabby crustacean shoves the anemone in its face. Nice! Because its hands are always full, this crackpot crab has to eat with its feet.

At the other end of the size scale are paltry pea crabs. They live inside mussel and oyster shells, picking scraps of food off their gills. Of course, size isn't everything. What krill (small shrimps) lack in size, they easily make up in numbers. They swim about in enormous swarms, weighing up to ten million tonnes. These swarms are so huge they can be spotted by satellites in outer space. They're the staple food of many sea creatures, including fish, seals and mighty blue whales. And they may soon be on the menu for you, too – in Russia, krill is catching on fast. But krill cuisine is trickier than it sounds.

1 First catch some krill. And that's not easy. The biggest swarms live in the freezing Southern Ocean. Byeeee!

2 Process it quickly. Krill goes off very fast. Phwoar!

3 Then give it some flavour. Apart from being vaguely fishy, it doesn't taste of much.

KRILL

4 Last but not least, find something else for blue whales to eat. And make sure there's plenty of it...

If you're looking for a less long-winded lunch, what about lobster? Lobsters are so tasty that people are now their worst enemy! Lobsters are usually brown and speckled but when a chef chucks one into boiling water, it turns bright pink in just six minutes and is cooked and ready to eat. Cruel? Certainly one chef thought so. He tried to hypnotize his lobsters by rubbing their backs before he cooked them, so they wouldn't feel a thing.

Each autumn, thousands of American spiny lobsters trek hundreds of kilometres across the Atlantic seabed. They scurry along in single file, holding on, for safety, to the lobster in front. They travel day and night, up to 60 together, and can cover 50 kilometres without a rest. The aim of their amazing journey is to find fresh supplies of food. They can tell when it's time to get going because of a sharp drop in sea temperature that comes with the first winter storms. It's a long way to go to end up in the pot.

What on Earth are molluscs?

Molluscs aren't fish either. They're creatures like clams, cockles, oysters, squid and octopuses. Like crunchy crustaceans, many molluscs have hard shells to protect their soft, squishy bodies. But not all...

Nine meaty mollusc facts

1 The most massive mollusc is the Atlantic giant squid which can grow a mighty 16 metres long (that's 6 metres of body and 10 metres of terrible tentacles). No wonder it doesn't need a shell as well.

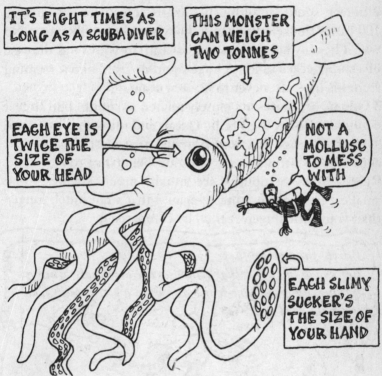

In days gone by, sailors were terrified by tales of a sea monster, large and mean enough to tip up a ship. Its name alone struck fear into their hearts. The blood-curdling kraken. Apparently, it had a mass of sucker-covered tentacles and a sharp, beaky mouth strong enough to bore through the broadest of beams. Sound familiar? Krakens were so big and solid that short-sighted sailors sometimes mistook them for islands and went ashore. One baffled bishop even set up an altar on a kraken's back and knelt down to say his prayers. Ooops! But what was this brutal beast, if it existed? Geographers think it must have been a giant squid, allowing for a bit of exaggeration.

2 In fact, squid are seriously sensitive creatures with nerves 100 times thicker than ours. They're not usually nasty. No way. The only known instance of death by squid was the case of a shipwrecked sailor. A huge squid dragged him screaming from his life-raft, never to be seen again.

3 Odious octopuses are closely related to squid. The largest octopuses live in the Pacific Ocean and measure more than 9 metres across their outstretched tentacles. That's right across your sitting-room. Imagine being hugged by that! Relax. Most octopuses are much, much smaller. The smallest has a 5-cm tentacle-span – that's not much longer than your little finger. A titch by comparison.

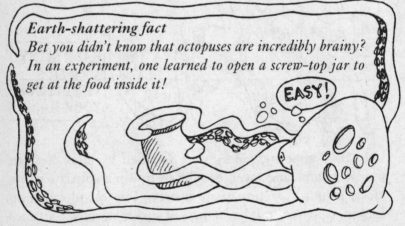

Earth-shattering fact
Bet you didn't know that octopuses are incredibly brainy? In an experiment, one learned to open a screw-top jar to get at the food inside it!

EASY!

4 The cuttlefish is another close cousin. These mild-mannered molluscs wear their shells on the inside, to help them float. You sometimes find them washed up on the

beach. They can also change colour, at the drop of a hat, by making tiny pigment (colour) cells in their skin shrink or grow. This helps them to hide, or attract a mate. If there's no place to hide, they squirt their enemies with thick, black ink while they make their getaway. Cunning.

5 The biggest seashell is the giant clam which hangs around near coral reefs. Some clam shells are so spacious you could hop in and have a nice, long bath. But forget any rumours about your legs getting trapped – the two halves of the shell close much too slowly to do any damage.

6 At high tide, a plough snail sucks water into its tube-shaped foot, then uses it as a surfboard to ride the waves on the lookout for food. When the tide goes out, it heads back to the shore and burrows into the sand.

7 To avoid being swept away with the tide, limpets cling to the rocks with a force 2,000 times their own weight. When the tide goes out, they feed on the green algae which grows on the rocks, moving backwards and forwards across it like tiny lawnmowers.

8 For centuries seashells were used as money. In Africa, you paid 25 cowrie shells for a chicken and 2,500 for a cow. Cowrie shells were also used as jewellery, lucky charms, and even as mummies' eyes. When a king died, in some parts of Asia, nine cowries were stuffed into his mouth, for him to use in the next world. Nobles were worth seven cowries; common people just one.

9 And finally, mussels stick to rocks using short, fine, black threads, called their "beards". What's really weird is that the beards are squeezed out of their feet. Weirder still, people in Italy used to collect clumps of mussel beards and weave them into cloth because they felt nice and silky – and probably still do.

Do any of these creatures sound temptingly tasty? Would you know which ones are good enough to eat? Before you get out your knife and fork, try this test on your teacher. We wouldn't want you getting indigestion, now, would we?

Can you eat it?*

The creatures in this quiz are all named after types of food. Because that's what gutsy geographers think they look like. But that doesn't mean to say you can eat them all. Get your teacher to look at this list and say, YUM! for "Yes, I'd eat

that," and YUK! for "No way am I touching that!" (Bear in mind, though, that some people will eat anything…)
(*Not suitable for vegetarians or anyone allergic to shellfish. Sorry.)

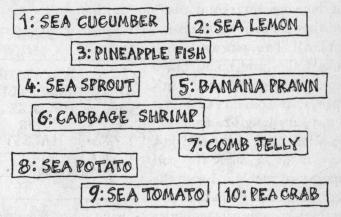

1: SEA CUCUMBER

2: SEA LEMON

3: PINEAPPLE FISH

4: SEA SPROUT

5: BANANA PRAWN

6: CABBAGE SHRIMP

7: COMB JELLY

8: SEA POTATO

9: SEA TOMATO

10: PEA CRAB

Answers:

1 YUM! The Japanese eat tonnes of the things. Sea cucumbers are small, sausagey creatures, that belong to the starfish and sea urchin family. They roam the seabed, sucking up scraps. If a hungry fish gets too close, they have a dramatic way of defending themselves. They shoot out streams of sticky guts, like strings of spaghetti, which tie the fish up in knots. Then they buzz off. Their guts grow back later, no problem. Fancy a mouthful?

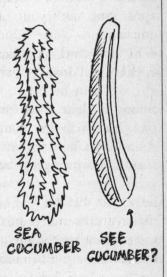

SEA CUCUMBER

SEE CUCUMBER?

2 YUK! Not recommended. Sea lemons are a type of sea slug (sea snails without seashells). When they're disturbed, they squirt out burning acid. And that's how they get their bitter name.

3 YUM! The pineapple fish looks yellow and spiny, like a pineapple and you can eat it (it's Japan, again!) but don't expect it to taste anything like fruit. On the other hand you could just keep it as a pet. Its odd appearance, combined with the fact that it glows in the dark (it's got two luminous patches under its chin), means you might well spot one in your nearest aquarium.

4 YUK! Sorry! A red herring.

5 YUM! Most prawns and shrimps can be eaten, though none of them tastes anything like bananas. In South-East Asia, banana prawns (and Indian prawns, tiger prawns and yellow prawns) are raised on huge fish "farms". These are massive saltwater ponds where the prawns are fed on specially nourishing algae to make them grow more quickly.

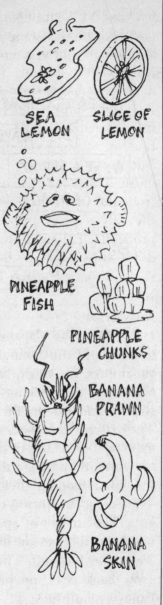

SEA LEMON

SLICE OF LEMON

PINEAPPLE FISH

PINEAPPLE CHUNKS

BANANA PRAWN

BANANA SKIN

6 YUK! No such thing. You get clam, cleaner, fairy and mud shrimps. You even get opossum and skeleton shrimps. But you don't get cabbage shrimps.

7 YUK! Comb jellies look like little glowing globules of jelly, floating through the open sea. But not the sort of jelly you mean. The name "comb" comes from the bristly fringes which the jelly wiggles and waves to propel itself along. Comb jellies don't sting at least, but their sticky tentacles snatch up their supper.

8 YUM! Sea potatoes are really sea urchins, harvested in some parts of the world (with their eggs) for food. Some people eat these with salad. But watch your fingers. Sea urchins are covered in sharp, spiky, often poisonous spines, which protect them from enemies. Including you. Sea potatoes also use their spines for burrowing into the sand to hide.

9 YUK! There are sea cucumbers and sea lettuces, but no sea tomatoes.

10 YUM! But you'd need an awful lot of them to fill you up.

NICE PLATE OF CABBAGE

COMB JELLY

JELLY WITH COMB

SEA POTATO

MASHED POTATO

PEA CRAB

CRAB PEE

Actually, pea crabs aren't very popular with some fishermen. They live inside edible mussels, spoiling the fisherman's catch.

If nothing so far tickles your tastebuds, how about eating like an Inuit? The Inuit live in the icy Arctic where they fish and hunt seals, walruses and whales, catching them with guns and harpoons. Seals are considered particularly tasty, especially stuffed with little auks (a type of sea bird). They're so important, in fact, that they've become part of Inuit folklore. This ancient Inuit legend explains how the seals came to be in the sea.

How the seals came to live in the sea *or* A fishy fingered tale

It's never easy being a girl, especially when you've got your dad going on and on at you all of the time. It's even worse when you're the goddess of the sea. Such a lot of responsibility. You never get any time to yourself.

Sedna was the goddess of the sea, and she lived with her father in a house on the shore. She was pretty and witty (and she knew it) and lots of men wanted to marry her. But snooty Sedna turned them all down. Then, one day, a handsome hunter paddled by in his canoe, dressed in splendid furs.

"Follow me," he said to Sedna. "To the land of the birds,

216

where no one goes hungry. Where you'll lie on warm bearskins inside my tent. And your cup will never run dry. Blah! blah! blah!" (Blokes in furs go on a bit.)

How could a girl refuse? Sedna had never seen anyone so handsome in all her life. What was she to do? Her heart said one thing; her head another. The handsome hunter was waiting. Suddenly, she made up her mind and leapt into the canoe, and they paddled off into the sunset together...

Now, the handsome hunter wasn't really a hunter. He was a sea bird spirit disguised as a man. But he'd fallen madly in love with Sedna and wanted to keep her, no matter what. So he kept his mouth (or beak) firmly shut. When Sedna finally found out the truth, she cried and cried for days on end, and wished that she was dead. Then, one day, when the sea bird was out, Sedna's dad turned up at the door. He'd come to take her home again, warm bearskins or no warm bearskins.

When the sea bird returned and looked for his wife, she was nowhere to be seen. Bravely, the wind broke the bad news. And before you could say "Sedna, come home, I may be a simple sea bird but I love you!", he'd changed into a human and hopped into his canoe. He soon caught up with Sedna and her dad. And he begged and begged her to come back home. But her father hid her in the bottom of his little boat and wouldn't let the hunter anywhere near her.

"Right," said the hunter. "I'll show you," he said. What did he do? He turned right back into a sea bird, spread his wings, and, croaking wildly, flapped away to get help from his spirit friends. Suddenly, a terrible storm blew up and swept across the ocean – the spirits were angry on the sea bird's behalf. Somebody would have to pay. Sedna's poor dad was scared to death. He'd feared the spirits all of his life and was hardly likely to stop fearing them now. There was only one thing for it, and he knew it – to make things better, he'd have to sacrifice his precious daughter to the sea. So, he picked her up and … chucked her overboard! Just like that.

Trying desperately to keep her head above water, Sedna gripped the side of the boat as tightly as she could. But her spirit-fearing father would not be put off. He picked up an axe and neatly chopped off her fingers so she couldn't hold on, no way!

Slowly but surely, Sedna sank beneath the waves but, amazingly, her fingers survived. And they turned into the seals, whales and walruses which live in the sea today. Then the storm died down and the sea grew calm and the spirits were contented. Sedna's dad made his sad way home, trying to put the whole thing behind him. But later that night, the highest tide ever seen covered the shore and swallowed him up, house and all, and carried him down to the depths of the sea. There he met his daughter again. What she said when she saw him is anybody's guess.

Now, if the Inuit want to make sure that they have plenty of seals and walruses to catch, one of them goes into a deep, deep trance. In his mind's eye, he travels down to the bottom of the sea to ask Sedna to send them good hunting. And sometimes she does, and sometimes she doesn't.

Oil and other ocean spoils
(BUT WATCH OUT FOR THE PIRATES)

Now, forget for a moment about fish, crabs, molluscs and seals. There's other stuff down under that you could put to good use. From salt to seaweed, sunken treasure to shipwrecks, pearls to precious metals, the sea is full of valuables. Some are horribly hard to find. Take gold, for example. There's masses of gold hanging around in sea water – about seven million tonnes in total. That's enough for everyone in the world to have a good, big chunk each. But getting it out is another story. Other things are easier to extract. Oil is one of the great ocean spoils…

1 One-fifth of all the oil we use comes from under the sea. Here's how it got there, and how we found it:
a) Millions of years ago, the sea was full of tiny plants and animals.

b) When they died, their bodies sank to the seabed.

c) They were buried under layers of sand and mud.

d) The sand and mud turned into rock …

e) … and squashed the bodies into thick, gungy oil.

f) This seeped upwards until it was trapped by harder rock above.

g) Millions of years passed. Then along came some geologists – scientists whose job is to study rocks. Geologists can guess where oil lies by looking carefully at the structure of the rocks on the seabed. Clever.

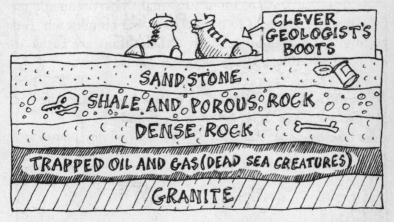

h) In order to be absolutely sure there is oil they have to drill a test hole. If they strike lucky, they're away, and can build a proper oil rig, with a pipeline that pumps the oil to a refinery on land. Supplies are brought on board and there's plenty of work for plenty of people.

i) An unlucky strike means going back to stage **g)** and trying again … and again, and again. Not so clever.

The world's main offshore oil fields are in the Middle East, the USA, Central and South America and the North Sea. Oil was first found under the North Sea in the 1960s. And what a fabulous find! A staggering 3.2 million barrels of oil are pumped out of the North Sea each day, and it's worth millions and millions of pounds. A single rig pumps up enough oil in a day to fill 70,000 cars with petrol.

2 Great as it seems, the oil isn't going to last for ever. And stocks are starting to run low. So what can we do? Well, there are other ways of finding energy from the sea. One idea is to collect the power of the tides and turn it into electricity. There's also Ocean Thermal Energy Conversion – that's a bit of a mouthful, so you can call it OTEC for short. The idea here is that scientists can use the difference in temperature between warm water on the surface of the sea and colder water deeper down to make electricity. In fact, OTEC sites are already working well in Hawaii, Japan, Florida and Cuba.

4 Why not season your seaweed with a pinch of sea salt? We eat six million tonnes of the stuff a year. In hot countries, collecting salt is easy. You dig a big, shallow pool along the coast and call it a salt pan. Then wait around for the tide to come in. The sea fills the pans, then the water evaporates (dries up) in the sun, and you're left with a layer of salt. Simple!

5 Taking the salt out of seawater can be useful in other ways too. In hot, dry desert countries such as those around the Persian Gulf in the Middle East, there are huge desalination plants (that's factory-type plants, not the green, leafy variety) along the coast. Here salt is extracted, leaving clean, fresh water for drinking. Brilliant.

Earth-shattering fact
Did you know that the finest fertilizer isn't seaweed, or horse poo, or even mouldy old teabags around your roses (honestly!). It's unsavoury seabird poo! Cormorant droppings, or ghastly guano (gwaano), are 50 times more fertile than horse poo. And smellier! So many cormorants once nested along the coast of Peru that the guano was deep enough to bury a house. Phew!

6 For deep-sea spoils, dive to the bottom of the great Pacific Ocean. It's covered in billions of dirty black lumps. They're called manganese nodules (nodule is a posh word for lump, that's all). Inside one of these nautical nodules you'll also find iron, nickel and copper. They've got a weird way of growing: over millions of years, layers of metal stick to a shark's tooth or a clump of sand, and that's it. They can be as small as a golfball to the size of a football. So all you have to do is collect them up and make your fortune. The big question is, how? Scientists are hoping that a machine which works a bit like a gigantic vacuum cleaner, and is carried by ship, will do the trick.

Pearls, pearls, pearls

If you really want to spoil yourself, treat yourself to a string of pearls. Pearls are one of the most precious ocean spoils. First, you'll have to find an irritable oyster. Why? Well, oysters, clams and mussels sometimes get pesky parasites inside their shells. You know when you've got an itch right in the middle of your back, always just out of reach? That's how annoying it can be. What do you think they do?
a) Rub up against a sea urchin's spines?
b) Smother it with mother-of-pearl?
c) Ignore it and hope it goes away?

The answer is b). The oyster tries the smother the itch with mother-of-pearl, or nacre (naker), the shiny stuff that lines its shell. And it works like a dream. But there's more. It can take years, true, but eventually, little by little, the nacre builds up into a gleaming, round pearl.

Pearls are not always pearly white. Far from it. They can be pink, purple, green, grey, or even black. And they come in

225

a wide range of sizes. The biggest pearl ever came from a huge giant clam. It was the size of a watermelon, but brain shaped! And it had a strange story to go with it.

Legend says that the pearl started life some 2,500 years ago, when a Chinese philosopher, Lao-Tzu, placed a small lucky charm inside a clam shell. Don't ask me why.

Inside the clam, the pearl started to grow.

Sometime in the 1500s, pearl and shell were caught in a typhoon and lost ... until a deep-sea diver found them again 400 years later.

The pearl was given to a Muslim chief who sold it to an American archaeologist. It recently went on sale again, for the earth-shattering sum of ... £20 million!

People who gaze into the pearl are said to see the faces of the Buddha, Confucius (another Chinese philosopher) and old Lao-Tzu himself.

Today, pearls are very big business. The bigger, rounder, shinier ... and pinker (that's the costliest colour), the better. But natural pearls are horribly expensive, because it's so tricky getting them out of the sea. Pearl-divers of old risked their lives every time they went to work. Their equipment was horribly basic – a nose clip, a basket and a weighted rope for lowering them to the seabed. They didn't have tanks of air to breathe – they just dived until they ran out of breath. Perilous! Prising open a clam and spying a pearl inside must be a magical moment. But is it worth risking your life for? Hardly. It wasn't the divers who made all the money – they got peanuts for their pearls.

As demand for pearls grew, the son of a Japanese noodle-seller had a brilliant idea. No more lives need be put in danger. He invented "cultured" pearls. No, it didn't mean they'd read more books or had better table manners than ordinary pearls. What happens is this:

1 An official oyster-irritator opens an oyster...

2 …and slips a slither of shell (usually mussel) inside.

3 Then he closes the shell, puts it back in the sea and waits.

4 The shell smothers the itch with nacre, then…

5 …three years later, the shell is opened, and, hey presto!, inside is a beautiful pearl.

Some far-fetched facts about oysters and pearls

1 Is your pearl real or fake? Try this test. Gently rub the pearl along the front of your teeth. It'll feel gritty if it's natural or cultured. If it's smooth, bad luck. It's a fake.

2 Powdered pearl was once used in love potions (and in

cures for madness). Other people think that eating oysters makes you...

a) taller?

b) brainier?

c) sick?

3 Pearl-divers in the Pacific had an ingenious way of taming sharks. To give themselves time to collect the pearls, they sent the sharks into a trance by ... "kissing" them on the nose. Not a problem with a nerdy old nurse shark. But kissing a tiger shark could be your last big adventure!

4 Oysters sometimes grow on trees. Honestly. That's because baby oysters like something to cling to, so branches are lowered into the water to give them a perch. After two or three months, the branches are brought up and the oysters bunged into barrels which are sunk back into the sea. Then you still have a long wait before the pearls are finally ready.

5 Dirty water can cause havoc with poor old oysters. In Japan, oysters have to have a good, regular wash to keep them pearly clean.

6 Not every oyster makes a pearl. That's what makes it so exciting...

Terrors of the high seas

At least oyster farmers make an honest living. Which is more than can be said of pirates of old. Their idea of ocean spoils was boarding a passing merchant ship, tying up or gruesomely killing the crew, and making off with as much lovely loot as they could carry. They were mad, bad and dangerous to know. But they didn't care. They wanted gold and they wanted it NOW.

Teacher teaser
Would your teacher make a good pirate? Ask her this cunning question as a test.

The terrible tale of Bonny and Read *or* Anything boys can do, girls can do better!

Of all the perilous pirates who roamed the high seas, two of the ghastliest were girls. Anne Bonny and Mary Read. They were awful enough apart. Together, they were deadly. This is the story of their hair-raising lives, and their sticky ends…

In those days, women were banned from pirate ships. If they were found on board, they were killed, along with anyone who had helped them. The only way for women to become pirates was to disguise themselves as men. And this is exactly what our horrible heroines did.

Mary Read was born in Plymouth, England, in 1690 and spent most of her girlhood dressed as a boy. Why? Well, Mary's granny had pots of cash and Mary's mother wanted a share of it. So she tricked poor old granny into leaving her money to Mary. But she had to pretend that Mary was a rosy-cheeked boy because granny *hated* girls!

By the age of 14, Mary had had enough. She left home and ran away to sea. Still dressed as a man, she fought in the army at Flanders, Belgium, then fell in love with a handsome soldier (he'd seen through her disguise). Did they live happily ever after? No, they didn't. The handsome soldier fell ill and died, leaving Mary with a broken heart. Sadly, she took to sea once more in a merchant ship, bound for the calming Caribbean Sea.

Meanwhile … Anne Bonny's life was taking just as strange a turn as Mary's. Her dad was a wealthy Irish lawyer but settling down, like a well-brought up girl should, wasn't Anne's style. By the age of 16, she had a taste for adventure. She ran off and married a sailor who was handsome but weak and the pair hitched a lift on a pirate ship which was also bound for the Caribbean. As soon as she clapped eyes on him, Anne fell in love with the ship's dashing captain, "Calico" Jack Rackham.

He got his nickname from his stripy, calico trousers – his absolute pride and joy. He was cruel, ruthless (quite possibly bearded) and … utterly irresistible! Anne ditched the sailor, donned cabin boy's clothes and joined dashing Calico Jack and his crew. (Calico knew Anne was a girl but he wasn't going to let on.)

One day, a fine merchant ship came sailing towards them. "Board!" growled Calico Jack. He was a man of few words.

The pirates captured the ship and forced a Dutch sailor,

young Mark Reid, to join their band. Soon Anne grew tired of Calico Jack (and his terrible trousers) and fell in love with mysterious Mark. Who didn't seem interested, for some strange reason.

It wasn't long before the truth came out – Mark was Mary, and Anne was not really a cabin boy. With their secret safe, the two joined forces and became the most famous double act since South China and Sea. They were by far the fiercest fighters in Calico's crew, and by far the best at cursing and swearing. In fact, their meanness put the men to shame. In 1720, when the ship was finally captured, only Mary and Anne stayed on deck to fight. The rest of the crew, who were rolling drunk (including clapped-out Calico), ran away and hid below deck.

This time, though, their luck was out. They were captured and tried for piracy, found guilty and sentenced to death. Calico Jack and his men were hanged. On the night before he went to the gallows, Anne visited him in his cell.

"If you'd fought like a man," she shouted, "you'd not be about to hang like a dog!" That told him.

Anne and Mary were spared the execution because both were expecting babies.

"My lord, we plead our bellies," they said in their defence.

They had a lucky escape. But Mary died later in prison. Anne survived, but vanished without trace, though it probably wasn't very long before she'd fallen in love all over again.

Piracy by the rules

By being women, Anne and Mary were breaking one of the first rules of piracy. And there were plenty of pirate rules. Pirates swore them on a Bible (or an axe) before setting out on a voyage. Would you have been able to stick to the rules?

1 You will have an equal say in the ship's running and an equal share of food and strong drink (except in emergencies).

2 You will get a fair share of the spoils. But if you steal from the ship, you'll be marooned (being left on your own in the middle of nowhere). If you steal from another man, you'll have your ears and nose cut off and be thrown overboard.

3 Gambling for money is strictly forbidden.

4 All lights and candles must be out by eight o'clock. If you want to stay up drinking, you can sit on deck in the dark.

5 You must keep your sword, cutlass and pistols clean, primed and ready for action.

6 Women are absolutely banned on board. Under no circumstances whatsoever. On pain of death.

7 The punishment for abandoning ship in battle is death or marooning.

8 Fighting on board is strictly forbidden. Any quarrels will be settled on shore by pistol or sword, as follows…

a) Stand back to back.

b) When the quartermaster gives the word, turn and fire.

c) If you both miss the target (i.e. each other), go back to stage **a)** and try again with your cutlasses (swords).

d) The first to draw blood is the winner.

9 You cannot leave the ship until your share's worth £1,000. (Note: You could bump up your pay by getting injured. Anyone who lost a limb in the course of duty got 800 pieces of eight. The going rate for losing an eye was 100 pieces of eight.)

10 It pays to get promoted. The captain and quartermaster receive double shares. The master gunner and boatswain one and a half shares; officers one and a quarter, and everyone else one each.

Perilous pirates today

You're probably thinking, phew, it's a good job all that stuff's ancient history! Well, sadly, that's where you're wrong... All the following pirate attacks happened in the last ten years. In fact, about 150 attacks are reported each year, especially in the perilous seas around Asia, Africa and South America. But the real total may be twice that number, and growing all the time. Today's pirates are in it for money, valuables and other goods to sell. And they don't care how they get it. The situation has got so serious that the International Maritime Bureau (IMB) set up a centre in Malaysia for monitoring pirates and their activities. It relies on information from ex-members of pirate gangs which is then passed on to shipping companies to warn them to protect their cargoes. It's a horribly risky business all round. And the details must be kept top secret.

PIRATE ATTACKS-TOP SECRET FILES

DATE OF ATTACK: December 1992

LOCATION: Java Sea, off Indonesia (Pacific Ocean)

SHIP: Baltimar Zephir

DETAILS OF ATTACK: Armed pirates board the ship at night, they take over the ship as the crew tries to hide. The British captain's SOS call is ignored by the passing ships who claim it is too dangerous to sail to his rescue. The pirates shoot the captain and first mate dead, steal the crew's valuables and make off in a small speed boat.
They are never caught.

DATE OF ATTACK: January 1993

LOCATION: South China Sea (Pacific Ocean)

SHIP: East Wood

DETAILS OF ATTACK: The ship, en route from Hong Kong to Taiwan, is seized by 30 machete-wielding pirates, and the captain is ordered to sail towards Hawaii. The 500 Chinese passengers are persuaded to pay the pirates £10,000 each, in return for visas to enter the USA, and the chance of a better life. Neither of which they get.

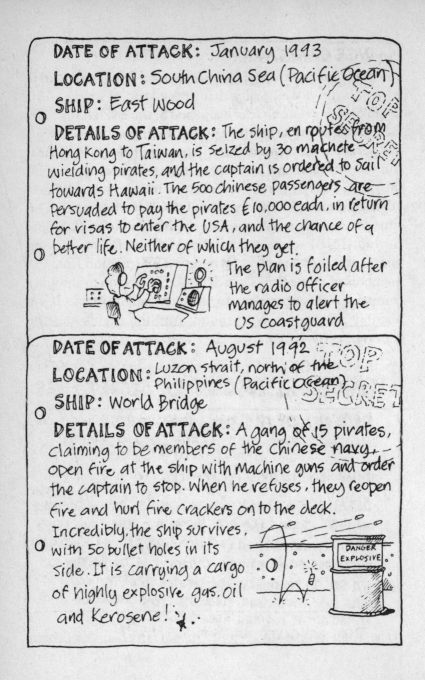

The plan is foiled after the radio officer manages to alert the US coastguard

DATE OF ATTACK: August 1992

LOCATION: Luzon Strait, north of the Philippines (Pacific Ocean)

SHIP: World Bridge

DETAILS OF ATTACK: A gang of 15 pirates, claiming to be members of the Chinese navy, open fire at the ship with machine guns and order the captain to stop. When he refuses, they reopen fire and hurl fire crackers on to the deck. Incredibly, the ship survives, with 50 bullet holes in its side. It is carrying a cargo of highly explosive gas, oil and kerosene!

DANGER EXPLOSIVE

DATE OF ATTACK: August 1991

LOCATION: Malaysian Coast (Pacific Ocean)

SHIP: Springstar

DETAILS OF ATTACK: 25 pirates armed with automatic rifles, hijack the ship, shoot dead the chief officer and dump his body overboard. They lock the crew in their quarters for two days, and make off with Springstar's cargo — £1·5 million worth of electronic goods.

These are later sold illegally in Singapore.

DATE OF ATTACK: September 1995

LOCATION: Gulf of Thailand (Pacific Ocean)

SHIP: Anna Sierra

DETAILS OF ATTACK: The ship is sailing from Bangkok to Manila with a cargo of sugar worth £2·7 million. Just after midnight, it is hijacked by 30 armed, masked men. The terrified crew are put into dinghies and set adrift without supplies. (They are later rescued by Vietnamese fishermen.) The pirates repaint the ship and rename it Arctic Sea, then they sail it to China where they sell the stolen sugar. By September the ship has been tracked down and the pirate crew captured.

True, some pirates do get away with it. But not all of them.

Modern-day pirates have to be careful. One was caught out when he left his mobile phone behind on the ship he'd just robbed. The police made a few calls and managed to track him and his gang down.

Of course, none of these deeds of derring-do, ancient or modern, would have been possible without … ships. So, all aboard, me hearties, for the next leg of your horrible voyage.

Ships. Where on Earth would we be without them? Sitting at home, high and dry, maybe? For centuries, people have messed about in boats, gone fishing in them, explored the world in them, set off on daring voyages of trade and discovery, even pillaged, plundered and conquered in them. Without ships and boats, Columbus would never have discovered America. No one would ever have made a film about the *Titanic*. And you'd never have tasted a bag of crisps. (Potatoes were brought over from South America in the 16th century. By ship.) Ships started off as simple canoes which were handy for crossing streams and things. Since then, they've got bigger, better and sturdier for travelling much, much further afield. Here are just some of the ships that have made history.

Ships that made a splash!

7,000 BC(ish) The first boat is made from a pine log (not to be confused with a ship's log) in Holland. Some horrible geographers say it isn't a ship at all. What do they think it is?

a AN ANCIENT COFFIN?

b AN ANCIENT SLEDGE? WHEEEEE!

c AN ANCIENT COOKING POT?

How to make a dug-out canoe

You will need:

a tree trunk (the straighter the better)

an axe

some planks

lots of patience

What to do:

1 Chop the tree down (ask permission first).

2 Hollow out the middle with your axe.

3 Turn it upside-down and hold it over a fire. This will open it up so you can sit in it. (You might need help with this bit.)

4 Put a couple of planks inside for seats.

5 Start paddling!

3,000 BC   The ancient Egyptians invent sails. They are made from reeds and are square (the sails, that is, not the ancient Egyptians).

2,300 BC   The ancient Egyptians invent the navy too. They send it on a couple of expeditions to conquer new lands and do a bit of trade in luxury goods like cedar wood.

*c.*333 BC	Alexander the Great explores the depths of the Aegean Sea in a glass barrel. So we're told.
AD 800	The Vikings build longships. These are long, narrow warships which are super-fast for launching surprise attacks, and super-light for carrying up rivers. This means the vile Vikings can terrorize more places than ever. To scare their enemies, the ships are given nasty names like *Long Serpent* or *Black Raven of the Wind*. And have fierce-looking dragons carved on the front of them.

900	The Chinese invent ships with several sails instead of one which makes them go much faster. They also invent rudders for steering.

1400	Three-masted ships are built in Europe. With even more sails, they can go even further and even faster.

1620	Cornelius van Drebbel of Holland builds the first submarine. Basically, it's a wooden barrel covered

in leather. He rows it up the River Thames in London, underwater.

1783   A French nobleman, the Marquis Jouffroy d'Abbans, invents the steamboat. For the next 100 years, steam power rules the waves.

1820s   Clipper ships are built in America to carry tea and wool. They get their name because they "clip" so much time off journeys.

1885   The first oil tanker is launched. Today's supertankers are the biggest ships afloat. A ULCC (Ultra Large Crude Carrier) can carry 500,000 tonnes of oil.

Earth-shattering fact
In February 1996, a smallish oil tanker (by oil tanker standards) called Sea Empress, ran aground off the coast of Wales and leaked a lethal 72,500 tonnes of oil. It smothered 1,300 sq. km of sea in filthy goo, coated 200 km of coastline and killed thousands of birds, fish and seals. Cleaning up the mess will take years and years.

1955   The world's first nuclear-powered submarine, USS *Nautilus*, is built in the USA. In its first two years, it travels 99,800 kilometres without having to stop and refuel. In 1958, it becomes the first ship to reach the North Pole (by sailing there under the ice).

1955   British inventor, Christopher Cockerell invents the hovercraft. He stumbles across the idea one day, while messing about with a coffee tin, some cat food, a bit of a hoover and some scales. Honestly!

1960s   The first ROVs (unmanned Remote-Operated Vehicles) are launched. They are used for exploring the best bits of the deep sea.

1990   SeaCat, the world's biggest catamaran, a boat with two hulls, is launched in Britain. (A hull is the nautical name for a ship's body.) It is twice as fast as a passenger ferry.

With all those ships sailing back and forth, there's bound to be the odd collision. In fact, the Straits of Dover in the English Channel are so overcrowded, the ships have to stay in lanes, like cars on a motorway. But no matter how carefully boats are designed and journeys are planned, accidents will happen. Here's one you've probably heard about before...

That sinking feeling – the terrible tale of RMS *Titanic*

Going back in time a bit...

On the evening of 14 April 1912, all was quiet on RMS *Titanic*, the biggest, most luxurious liner ever built. She was on the fourth day of her maiden voyage from Southampton to New York, sailing across the North Atlantic, with 2,201 people on board. One of the passengers asked about safety.

No one had any reason to doubt him. The *Titanic* was built of the finest steel, with no expense spared. She was 260 metres long and nine decks high, taller than a ten-storey building. She had four huge funnels, each wide enough to drive a train through, and three huge anchors, weighing as much as eight cars each. There had never been a finer ship.

At midday on Wednesday 10 April 1912, the *Titanic* slid majestically out of Southampton harbour. A brass band played and cheering crowds lined the quayside to wave the ship off. Her passengers, among them some of the world's richest people, settled down to enjoy themselves – the ship had its own swimming-pool, tennis courts, palm garden, Turkish baths, billiard hall, dark room for amateur photographers: you name it, it had it. The *Titanic* had everything. For four blissful days, things couldn't have looked easier.

Then, suddenly, on Sunday 14 April, things started to go horribly wrong…

Sunday, 14 April
During the day, the weather gets worse and the *Titanic* receives seven ice warnings from other ships.
11.40 p.m. The lookouts report an iceberg dead ahead. The ship swings hard to port (left) to avoid it. But it moves too late. The iceberg scrapes the ship's starboard (right) side, gashing a hole in the hull. On the upper decks (first class), all that the passengers notice is a grinding noise and a slight jolt. Many of them don't even wake up. On the lower decks, it's a different story…
11.50 p.m. Water pours into the front of the ship, and keeps rising.

The ship is brought slowly to a juddering halt.

Monday, 15 April

12.00 a.m. The extent of the damage now becomes clear – unbelievably, the ship is sinking. A distress signal is sent out on the radio. The captain orders the lifeboats to be uncovered. But it turns out that the *Titanic* only has enough lifeboats for half its passengers and crew.

12.25 a.m. The situation gets worse. Orders are given to load women and children into the lifeboats first. The men are left on deck, waving goodbye to their loved ones. Some women refuse to leave their husbands. Hopes are raised when a ship's lights come into view. But the ship turns and steams away again. It doesn't even seem to have seen them.

12.35 a.m. Two other ships, the *Carpathia* and the *Mount Temple*, about 80 kilometres away, pick up the *Titanic*'s SOS and head towards her at full speed.

12.45 a.m. The first lifeboat is lowered, less than half full. And the first of eight distress flares are fired.

1.00–2.00 a.m. More lifeboats leave. The ship is now tilting steeply. Hundreds of people remain on board. The ship's band strikes up a cheery tune to keep their spirits up.

2.17 a.m. The captain gives the order to abandon ship.
2.18 a.m. The ship's lights blink once, then go out for good.

Two minutes later, at 2.20 a.m., the *Titanic* turned on her end and sank...

At 4.00 a.m., the *Carpathia* finally reached the terrible scene and rescued more than 700 people from the lifeboats. But many passengers died floating in their lifejackets in the icy sea. A total of 1,490 lives were lost.

Some risky reasons why the *Titanic* sank

1 She hit an iceberg. In April, in the North Atlantic, icebergs and pack ice are common hazards for ships. The iceberg that sank the *Titanic* was small and dark, and seven-eighths lay hidden underwater. By the time the lookouts spotted it, it was already much too late.

2 Despite seven ice warnings, the *Titanic* was travelling at full steam ahead. Far too fast for such icy seas.

3 The ship was declared watertight by its builders. It had a double-layered bottom and 15 watertight compartments making up the area below decks. The idea was that, if even three or four flooded, the *Titanic* would still be able to float. As it happened, water poured into the first five compartments, then spilled over into the others. The ship was doomed.

4 Did the collision trigger a massive explosion in the ship's coal bunker (The *Titanic* was a steam ship, powered by coal.), blowing a hole in the side? Some experts think so. Strangely, the ship had set sail from Southampton with one of its bunkers on fire.

5 Stranger still, some people blamed an Egyptian mummy being shipped across to America. Nicknamed "Shipwrecker", it was said to be cursed. Rumour had it that, just as the captain gave the order to abandon ship, the mummy appeared on deck. Spooky.

Whatever the reason for the *Titanic* tragedy, going to sea would never be the same again. It was safety first from now on. By law, ships had to carry enough lifeboats for everyone on board. Emergency and safety drills were improved. And lookouts had to have regular eye tests. And the watertight bulkheads now had to extend upwards right to the weather deck. In the North Atlantic, the International Ice Patrol was set up to warn ships of hazards. And no one ever claimed that a ship was unsinkable ever again. They didn't dare.

Is a sailor's life for you?

But what about the people who had to sail all these ships? You might think your life is horrible, what with too much homework and too little pocket money. But is it really bad enough to make you run away to sea? Count your lucky stars you weren't a sailor in days gone by. Here's an example of what you might have had for your supper.

On the mouldy menu today…

MAIN COURSE: ∿
LOBSCOUSE
ROPE-YARNS OR BABIES' HEADS
SERVED WITH
TRAIN SMASH & GALLY PEPPER

∿ DESSERT: ∿
FIGGY-DUFF
OR
DANDY-FUNK

Roughly translated, that's…

MAIN COURSE:

RAISIN BISCUIT AND SALT-MEAT STEW
TINNED MEAT OR CANNED MEAT PUDDING

SERVED WITH:

TINNED TOMATOES AND SMUTS (SMUTS WERE ASHES
FROM THE FIRE THAT FELL INTO THE COOKING POTS.
NOBODY BOTHERED TO PICK THEM OUT AGAIN.)

DESSERT:

RAISIN PUDDING
OR
BROKEN BISCUIT PIE (WITH THE ODD WEEVIL – THAT'S
A SMALL CREEPY CRAWLY THROWN IN FOR FLAVOUR.)

Rum rations
No wonder sailors looked forward to their daily ration of
grog (rum and water). They needed it to wash their Babies'
Heads down!

Sick as a sea dog

If the food didn't get you first, the seasickness might. Even the saltiest old sea dogs got seasick. Including Horatio Lord Nelson, Britain's best-known sailor. On his very first voyage, he was horribly seasick for months on end. And 30 years later, he was still being sick. (He also suffered from yellow fever, scurvy, malaria and bouts of depression, but that's another story…) It's the rocking motion of the boat that's the problem. It upsets your balance and confuses your brain. Which makes you feel sick. Is there a cure? Well, sort of. Many cures have been tried and failed. Staring straight ahead at the horizon can help. Or you can wear a seasickness wristband. The plastic button on the strap presses against a sensitive spot on your wrist and makes you feel better. At least, that's the theory… Most cures, unfortunately, just send you to sleep. Zzzzzzzz!

A British inventor, Sir Henry Bessemer, had a brilliant idea for beating seasickness on cross-channel steamships. He devised a "swinging saloon" which balanced on a central pivot and was meant to stay on an even keel, no matter how much the ship rocked and rolled. Sir Henry, who was always seasick himself, hoped to put a stop to it once and for all. Unfortunately, the saloon swung so violently that some people were seasick who'd never been seasick before!

251

Dreadful food and seasickness sound bad enough? Worse things can happen to a sailor...

Adrift on a raft

Imagine being all alone at sea. With only a seagull for company. You'd soon get hopelessly lonely and bored. The first week would be bad enough. But what on Earth would you do by week ten? Or 19? Someone who knew just how this felt was a young sailor, called Poon Lim, who proved one of the sea's greatest survivors. This is his real-life story...

On 23 November 1942, the SS *Ben Lomond*, a ship in the British Merchant Navy, was torpedoed by a German submarine in the Atlantic, some 565 miles west of Britain. It was the Second World War. Poon Lim was 25, he was the second steward on the ship – and he was the only one who survived the attack. His day had started off badly, and soon got worse. Before his ship sank, Poon Lim realized he needed to act, and fast. He grabbed a life-raft and some supplies and clambered on board. He had enough food and water for 50 days. Never in his wildest dreams did poor Poon

Lim imagine he'd be on board for more than a day or two.

But 50 days later, there he was. When his food ran out, Poon Lim had to live by his wits. He took the metal spring out of his pocket torch and shaped it into a fish-hook.

Then he ground up some biscuit crumbs into paste for bait and started fishing. Unfortunately, fish was all there was. For almost three months, Poon Lim lived on a diet of raw fish (and the odd slither of seagull), washed down with handfuls of rainwater.

Several times, Poon Lim was almost rescued. Almost, but not quite. Finally, on 5 April 1943, he was picked up by a fishing boat off the coast of Brazil. He'd spent a total of 133 days alone on his raft, a record that has never been broken. Amazingly, after all he'd been through, he only had a bit of tummy ache. Apart from that, he was fit and well. He was awarded the British Empire Medal for his incredible courage.

But when, some time later, Poon Lim applied to join the US Navy, he was turned down. Why do you think that was?

a) Because he couldn't swim.

b) Because he got seasick.

c) Because he had flat feet.

**Answer: Believe it or not, the answer is c). And Poon Lim might still have had problems today. When you join the modern-day Navy, you must have a medical to make sure that you're fit and healthy. And you can still fail if your feet are flat (or you suffer from colour blindness).

Do you have what it takes to join the Navy?

Fancy a life on the ocean waves? The good news is that the Navy today isn't quite as harsh as it used to be (although some sailors might say that the food is just as bad.) The bad news is that to get in, you have to pass some nasty nautical tests...

Stage 1: Have you got what it takes?

Answer the following questions – it's best to be honest! Are you:

a) Over 18? (If you're only 12, you'll have to wait. If you're 16 or 17, you'll need your parents' permission.)

b) Physically fit? (You'll soon be even fitter.)

c) Keen to learn? (If you're running away to the Navy to escape from school, forget it. You'll be kicking off your new career with eight weeks of hard training.)

d) Well educated? (Errr, if you're not sure, ask a teacher.)

e) Able to swim? (For obvious reasons!)

COULD I HAVE A WORD, PETERSON?

f) Good at ironing? (You'll have to learn fast. Your kit has to be kept in tip-top condition for inspection.)

g) Good at teamwork? (You'll be spending a lot of time with the same bunch of people – and that's not just in the daytime, you'll be sleeping in the same room as well.)

If you answered yes to most of these questions, go on to the next stage. If you've more nos than yeses, OK, you're excused, you can skip to the end of the chapter.

Stage 2: Have you got any brains?
See how naturally nautical you are by answering these real Navy entrance questions. But be quick. You've only got 15 seconds to answer question 1 and 2 and 30 seconds for question 3. On your marks, get set, go!

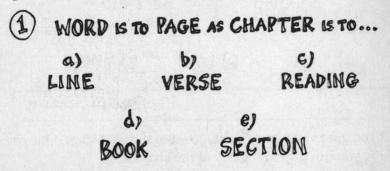

(1) WORD IS TO PAGE AS CHAPTER IS TO...

a) LINE   b) VERSE   c) READING

d) BOOK   e) SECTION

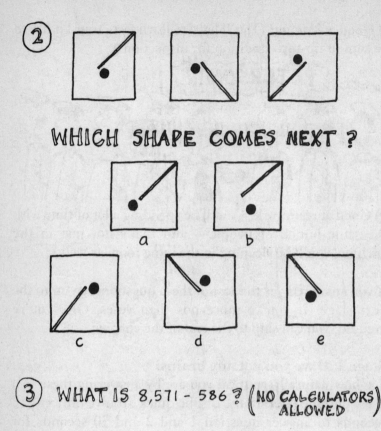

(2)

WHICH SHAPE COMES NEXT ?

a

b

c

d

e

(3) WHAT IS 8,571 - 586 ? (NO CALCULATORS ALLOWED)

A) 7,995   B) 8,015

C) 7,985   D) 8,085   E) 7,085

If you got two or more right, go on to the next stage. One or less, you can skip to the end of the chapter.

Stage 3: Have you got any muscles?

OK, so you don't have to be Mr or Miss Universe, but if you're the sort of person who'll do anything to get out of PE, you're heading for the wrong career. Parading, working out in the gym, cross-country running and assault courses are just a few of the exhausting exercises you'll be expected to enjoy.

You'll need a thorough medical examination, too. And you can fail if you suffer from:

But it all depends on what job you want to do (see below). For example, good eyesight is crucial for a pilot. Stands to reason.

Are you fighting fit? Then congratulations! You've passed! On with your eight weeks of training. It's a bit different from school, though. Your timetable's going to include learning how to tie ropes up in knots (or bends and hitches, as they're called at sea); how to march properly (and that's not as simple as it looks); how to keep your kit clean (no, you can't take your mum with you).

If you get through all this, you're ready for "trade" training which teaches you how to do a particular job. Here are a few you could choose from:

NOTICE BOARD

DIVER

WEAPONS INSTRUCTOR

NURSE

TRANSLATOR

SURVEYOR

SUB-CREW

MECHANIC

CHEF OR SHIP'S STEWARD

WRITER

ENGINEER

ACCOUNTANT

REWARD

HAS ANYONE SEEN THIS FISH?

DRUMMER OR BUGLER

PILOT

It can take a few weeks, or it can take years, but once you're through training, you're ready for action! Ah … didn't you realize, being in the Navy means if there's a war on, you'll probably be in the thick of things. Still want to join…?

What if you're happy being a land-loving lazybones, get terrible seasickness or are just plain scared? Well, you're in good company, there are plenty of us who don't fancy a life at sea. Maybe you'd rather read about adventure and excitement instead? Well, brace yourself. You're about to meet some of the greatest explorers in the whole history of the salty seas.

For thousands of years, intrepid explorers have sailed the seas in search of adventure. Some had specific adventures in mind, like discovering new lands or new places to trade. Others didn't know where they were going. They simply set off as the fancy took them.

The plucky Polynesians

The plucky Polynesians were exploring the vast Pacific Ocean over 2,000 years ago. Long before anyone else had heard of it. They loaded their huge dug-out canoes with people, plants and animals, and set off to find new islands to live on. Including New Zealand. And Easter Island. And Hawaii, to name but a few. They were born sailors, the Polynesians. And incredibly ingenious. They had to be. They didn't have charts, compasses, telescopes or any other mod cons to help them navigate. Instead they followed the sun, stars, clouds, and mysterious bundles of … sticks! Actually these stick maps were unbelievably useful. They were used for teaching budding sailors to find islands without actually seeing them. Even from 150 kilometres away.

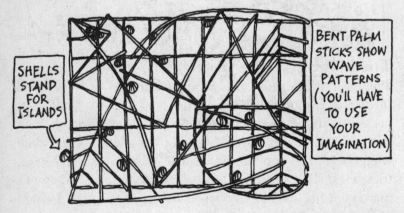

SHELLS STAND FOR ISLANDS

BENT PALM STICKS SHOW WAVE PATTERNS (YOU'LL HAVE TO USE YOUR IMAGINATION)

The intrepid Egyptians

In about 600 BC, Pharaoh Necho II of Egypt had a brilliant idea. Rather than build a canal through the desert, to link the Red Sea to the Mediterranean – that idea had to wait until 1859 when the Suez Canal was built, which cut thousands of kilometres off the voyage – he decided to sail right around Africa, from the east coast of Egypt to the north. Which was all very well but he had absolutely no idea just how big Africa was! He couldn't make the trip himself, what with ruling and what not. So he hired some sailors from nearby Phoenicia, complete with their own boats. And off they went. It wasn't long before they wished that they'd never heard of nutty Necho and his potty plan. It took one gruelling year to sail down the east coast of Africa, and another to sail up the west coast – a round trip of 25,000 kilometres. And then when they got back no one believed they'd really made it!

The globe-trotting Greeks

They weren't the only ones to feel fed up. Nobody believed the Greek explorer, Pytheas, either, when he got back from his sailing trip in the north Atlantic. People laughed when he said he'd seen seas covered in ice. "Don't be daft," they sniggered. "You don't get ice at sea." (Bit of a Titanic error, that one!) The year was 304 BC. Poor Pytheas. To make matters worse, nobody believed he'd sailed round Britain either (where?), although he described its "extremely chilly climate"! He spent the rest of his life trying to convince people he was telling the truth.

Who really discovered America?

Despite warnings that he'd fall off the edge of the world or be eaten alive by sea monsters, Christopher Columbus set sail from Spain in 1492 to discover America. He didn't mean to discover America. He was actually looking for a new route to Asia and he firmly believed that he'd found one. (In fact, he'd miscalculated the size of the Earth and made it a quarter too small. He obviously didn't allow for sea floor spreading. Remember that?) He even made his crew swear to go along with his story and say that America was Asia. Else he'd have their tongues cut out!

Some horrible geographers agree with Columbus. They don't think he 'discovered' America either. In fact, they lined up several other suspects who they thought had beaten him to it. These included:

TWO CHINESE EXPLORERS

PHOENICIANS

EGYPTIANS

CARTHAGINIANS

CELTS

AN IRISH MONK

SOME VIKINGS

AN AFRICAN KING

A WELSH PRINCE

Luckily for Columbus, no one's been able to find convincing proof for any of these claims. So it looks like you're stuck with Columbus. Who must have been really pleased when his newly-found continent was named after his friend, Amerigo Vespucci, Italian navigator, sailor and ex-pickle-seller.

In 1519, another ace explorer, Ferdinand Magellan, had a dream. To sail around the world. No one had ever done this before! Would he make it? Read on to find out...

The amazing adventures of Ferdinand Magellan (c.1480–1521)

Hardship on the high seas

1 Spain, August 1519. With five fine ships and a motley 280-man crew, Magellan sets out on the journey of a lifetime.

I THOUGHT WE WERE GOING THE OTHER WAY

2 The Atlantic, August–December 1519. The ships head west. Apart from stores and supplies, they take thousands of combs, mirrors, small brass bells and fish hooks to trade for food and safe passage.

3 Rio de Janeiro, December 1519. They stop off for two weeks in Rio where the sailors are treated like gods. For some reason, they don't want to leave.

4 February 1520. After weeks and weeks of sailing around getting nowhere, the choice is this – to go back to Rio for a rest? Or sail south to the Southern Ocean, then head west? Magellan votes to carry on. Not a very popular move.

5 Along the South American coast, March 1520. After another month of freezing cold weather and storms, things turn even nastier. Three ships mutiny. Magellan has two ringleaders beheaded, and the other marooned. That should teach 'em.

6 A bit further along the South American coast, October 1520. One ship is lost and another deserts, taking a third of the stores.

7 At the tip of South America, October 1520. Magellan discovers a channel which links the Atlantic to the perilous Pacific … he calls it the Straits of Magellan – big head! It takes 38 days to sail through.

8 The Pacific, October 1520–March 1521. Things go from bad to worse. There's been no sight of land for months. And the sailors are struck down by scurvy*, starvation and thirst.

*Note: A disease caused by not eating your greens. So watch it!

9 The Philippines, March 1521. At last, land ahoy. And the end of the line for mad old Magellan. He is caught poking his nose into a local war, and killed. One ship is abandoned. Two sail on.

10 The Moluccas, November 1521. At the famous Spice Islands (Indonesia), the ships load up with valuable cloves. Disaster strikes as one ship springs a leak and sinks.

11 The Indian Ocean, February–July 1522. The fifth and last ship, *Victoria*, sails on. Her captain is Juan Sebastian del Cano, a former mutineer. Times are tough. The food goes off in the heat; the water turns yellow and scummy. The ships' masts are snapped by storms.

12 Spain, September 1522. Three long years and 94,000 kilometres later, *Victoria* limps home, a total wreck. Of the original crew of 280, only 18 survive to tell the tale. At least they can boast that they're the very first people to sail around the world.

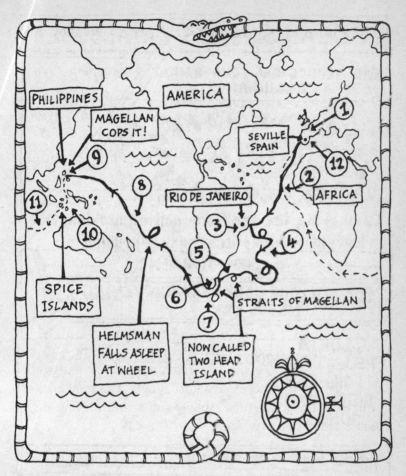

Latest equipment for explorers – hurry while stocks last!

Modern explorers are delving deeper than ever before. But they don't do the hard work themselves. Oh, no. Sometimes they don't even get their feet wet. They have lots of mod cons to help them out. Go on, give yourself a break. Meet Gloria, Jason, Kaiko and the gang. Check out these adverts…

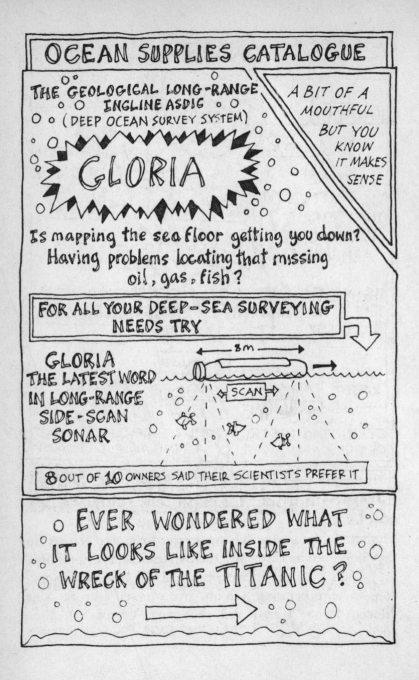

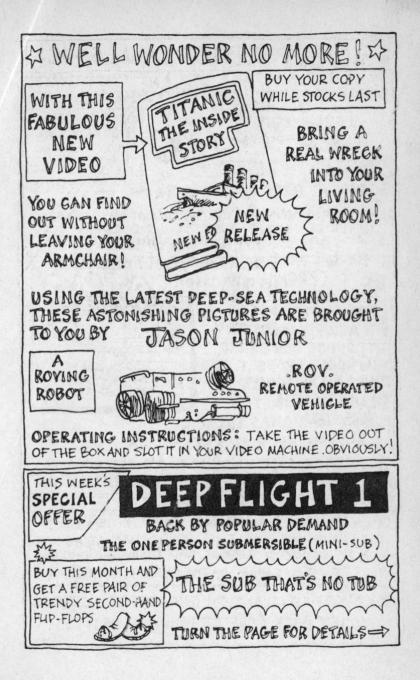

Joshua Slocum – going it alone

One man who'd have found these mod cons far too newfangled was Captain Joshua Slocum, the first person to sail solo around the world. (Even though he couldn't swim.) Here's how he might have described his adventures in his diary:

Dear Diary...

24 April 1895, Rhode Island, USA

At last! After months of hard work and high hopes, I finally set sail, in my faithful old oyster sloop, Spray. I remember the day I first saw her. A great pile of scrap in a field. No longer! Now she sails like a dream... where was I? oh yes... after months of hard work, spray and I set sail...

ME

SPRAY

January – February 1896

It's been a while since I last wrote. But things have been rather hectic. I spent longer in Buenos Aires (Argentina) than expected, having poor old Spray restocked and refitted. In January we set off again, heading for the Straits of Magellan. What a journey! Battered by one storm after another. Waves like you've never seen before, seas the colour of thunder. I thought we'd had it, <u>thunderous waves</u>; I can tell you. I just had time to drop the sails and batten down the hatches, when the storm hit like a cannon shot!

But Spray came good, that's my girl! We entered the straits on 11 February and dropped anchor in Chile three days later, for a well-earned rest. Lovely people, strange line in gifts; when we left five days later, they showered us with biscuits, smoked venison, a compass and several bags of...

Carpet tacks!

20 February 1896 (my birthday)

Fifty two again. No cards. No cake. No gifts. except for the carpet tacks, of course!

some time later I never want to see a pirate again. Verminous SCUMBAGS! That's twice we've been attacked in as many months! If it hadn't been for the carpet tacks, goodness knows where we'd be now. I took the precaution, before going to bed, of sprinkling them over the deck. Howls of pain woke me up at midnight. Next thing I knew, a great bearded brute was standing in front of me, bold as brass. It was Black Pedro himself, the scourge of the straits. Now, he may think he looks big, bad and ugly but I wasn't scared of him. Oh no. I pointed my gun at him, sneered (really quite nastily) and he ran off!

He turned up again next day, wanting to borrow my gun to shoot birds. Do I look like I was born yesterday? Instead I gave him a knife for carving canoes, (a nice, safe, occupation) and sat down to a hot bowl of venison stew. There's nothing like a hot meal after a difficult day.

April-May 1896

Things couldn't be better, with Black Pedro behind us, and the weather turning warmer, we spent a happy two weeks on the island of Juan Fernandez (off the Chilean coast). As I headed ashore, some local people came aboard. I offered them coffee and doughnuts, in case they were peckish. The doughnuts went down well, so well in fact, that I made a tidy sum in gold showing the locals how to bake them. A most pleasant place.

six months later

I shan't bore you with more tales of storms and torn sails, though there's been plenty of both. Having crossed the Pacific and Indian Oceans, we spent some days on the island of St Helena (in the South Atlantic) where the governor treated me like a long lost friend. As I was leaving he gave me a gift, to keep me company, he said and handed me a... GOAT! Worse than any pirate or storm, it chewed through its rope, my best sun hat, it also ate my charts and didn't give me a minute's peace. When we reached Ascension Island some weeks later, I put the wretched creature ashore and carried on alone. Bliss!

Hooray!

STILL CHEWING!

3 July 1898

Journey's end. Three long years and 140,028 km later, Spray and I reached home. What I'll do now, I have no idea. Certainly goat-keeping's out of the question. Perhaps I'll write a book...

J. Slocum

And this is what Joshua Slocum did. His epic account of his record-breaking voyage, *Sailing Alone Around the World*, became a bestseller. He spent the next ten years writing and giving lectures. People often asked why he'd gone in the first place but he was never quite sure of the answer. In 1909, he was off again, planning to sail down the Amazon River. He was never seen again.

Deepish deep-sea diving

If you want to explore the sea by yourself, the best thing to do is go diving. My advice for beginners would be to start off small with a snorkel and flippers. And don't freak out if you come face-to-face with a fish. It's probably far more frightened of you.

Apart from exploring, we divers also suss out shipwrecks, search for sunken treasure, take recordings and measurements, monitor wildlife, and do fiddly jobs, like repairing old oil rigs. But there is a bit of a problem. The longest people can dive for, just by holding their breath, is a paltry two minutes 45 seconds. Any longer and you'd starve your brain of oxygen, which could damage it. And that means you can only go a few metres down. To dive any deeper, you need to take an air supply with you. We scuba-divers strap tanks of air on our backs and breathe through a mouthpiece. (By the way, to be a scuba-diver, you'll need to take lessons first. You can't just plunge in, flippers first. Ask at your local swimming-pool.) Breathing ordinary air (mostly oxygen and nitrogen), you can dive to about 50 metres. Breathing a different mixture of gases (oxygen, nitrogen and helium – that's the gas used to fill airships), you can dive deeper, to about 300 metres. But...

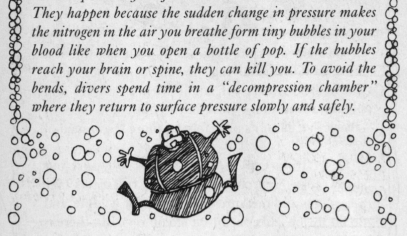

Cool clothes for deep-sea diving

Sadly, people aren't naturally nautical. To stay underwater for any length of time, we need all sorts of special clothes and equipment. Let me tell you how I pick the best diving gear for the job.

I'm about to dive into my first-ever modelling assignment. I tried three different diving suits – here are the pics, and my notes which tell you what I thought about each one.

Odious outfit No. 1

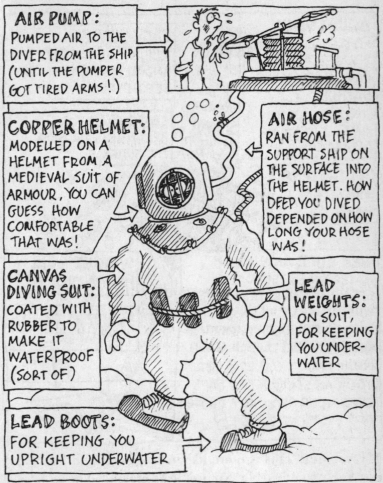

AIR PUMP: PUMPED AIR TO THE DIVER FROM THE SHIP (UNTIL THE PUMPER GOT TIRED ARMS!)

COPPER HELMET: MODELLED ON A HELMET FROM A MEDIEVAL SUIT OF ARMOUR, YOU CAN GUESS HOW COMFORTABLE THAT WAS!

AIR HOSE: RAN FROM THE SUPPORT SHIP ON THE SURFACE INTO THE HELMET. HOW DEEP YOU DIVED DEPENDED ON HOW LONG YOUR HOSE WAS!

CANVAS DIVING SUIT: COATED WITH RUBBER TO MAKE IT WATERPROOF (SORT OF)

LEAD WEIGHTS: ON SUIT, FOR KEEPING YOU UNDER-WATER

LEAD BOOTS: FOR KEEPING YOU UPRIGHT UNDERWATER

My verdict: Horribly heavy and cumbersome. Almost impossible to walk in or even stand upright. And what if my air hose got tangled up or broken? I could easily be strangled or suffocated. It doesn't bear thinking about.

Marks out of 10: 0

AQUALUNG: PORTABLE AIR TANK, STRAPPED TO MY BACK. ALSO CALLED **SCUBA:** (SELF-CONTAINED UNDERWATER BREATHING APPARATUS

FACE MASK: KEEPS OUT WATER AND HELPS ME TO SEE BETTER

SNORKEL: FOR BREATHING AIR NEAR THE SURFACE

MOUTHPIECE: SHOULD FIT SNUGLY

WET SUIT: AN ALL-IN-ONE WATERPROOF RUBBER SUIT. SEALED AT THE EXTREMITIES. YOU CAN WEAR THERMAL UNDIES FOR EXTRA WARMTH. **OR DRY SUIT:** EVEN WARMER. FOR DIVING IN COLDER WATER. YOU CAN SLIP THIS ONE ON OVER YOUR ORDINARY CLOTHES AND STEP OUT BONE DRY

WEIGHT BELT: FULLY ADJUSTABLE

FLIPPERS OR FINS: FOR THAT EXTRA KICK

My verdict: This is more like it. It's lovely and light, and extremely comfortable. No problems of tangled hoses here. I think it rather suits me, don't you? Just bear in mind that it takes a while to learn to use an aqualung and to regulate the flow of air. Otherwise you could get yourself in serious trouble.

Marks out of 10: 8½

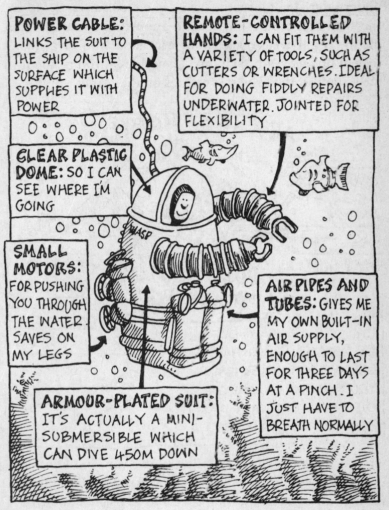

POWER CABLE: LINKS THE SUIT TO THE SHIP ON THE SURFACE WHICH SUPPLIES IT WITH POWER

REMOTE-CONTROLLED HANDS: I CAN FIT THEM WITH A VARIETY OF TOOLS, SUCH AS CUTTERS OR WRENCHES. IDEAL FOR DOING FIDDLY REPAIRS UNDERWATER. JOINTED FOR FLEXIBILITY

CLEAR PLASTIC DOME: SO I CAN SEE WHERE I'M GOING

SMALL MOTORS: FOR PUSHING YOU THROUGH THE WATER. SAVES ON MY LEGS

AIR PIPES AND TUBES: GIVES ME MY OWN BUILT-IN AIR SUPPLY, ENOUGH TO LAST FOR THREE DAYS AT A PINCH. I JUST HAVE TO BREATH NORMALLY

ARMOUR-PLATED SUIT: IT'S ACTUALLY A MINI-SUBMERSIBLE WHICH CAN DIVE 450M DOWN

My verdict: Wow! They don't come much smarter than this, do they? This is an absolute must for the serious diver. I love the hands. A bit pricey for me, but a pleasure to wear. **Marks out of 10: 10**

Whatever you're wearing, while you're dabbling about underwater, don't forget to have a good look around. Go on, the fish won't bite. On second thoughts, some of them might. You'll need to keep your wits about you. Are you all togged up and ready to jump? Good luck – you're about to meet some of the fishiest creatures on the planet…

DEEP, DARK and DANGEROUS

There are thousands of creatures in the oceans. But are they all as scary as you'd expect them to be? The answer is: well, some of them are. Others are even bigger and scarier than you'd imagine. Of course, size isn't everything. Some of the deadliest sea creatures are horribly small. And some of the biggest wouldn't hurt a fly. Take, for example, a big blue whale...

Ten reasons to give a blue whale a wide berth

1 Blue whales are the biggest animals that have ever lived. Ever! Bigger than dinosaurs! Over 30 metres long and 130 tonnes in weight (that's as heavy as 20 elephants). More like a submarine than a sea mammal.

FUNNY LOOKING WHALE!

2 A blue whale's tongue weighs three whole tonnes. (As much as a whole rhinoceros.) Luckily, the blue whale has got a very big mouth!

3 Blue whale blubber (that's the thick layer of fat under its skin) can weigh 30 tonnes. It keeps the whale warm, especially in the parky polar seas, and gives it a streamlined shape for swimming.

4 Even baby blues weigh two tonnes at birth. And they grow up unbelievably fast. By the time they're two, they weigh a whopping 50 tonnes.

5 Blue whales have very big eyes compared to ours, about the size of footballs. We don't know how well they can see with them, though.

6 In the wild, blue whales can live for 80–90 years. If they're left to get on with it. But tens of thousands have been hunted and killed for their meat, blubber and whalebone, so that at one time they almost disappeared altogether. Today, though, they're making a comeback.

7 Blue whales couldn't survive on land. They're just too bloomin' big. They'd need such huge legs that they'd never be able to walk. The only place that can support their great bulk is the sea...

8 They might have lived on land once, though. Some whales and dolphins did. But they took to the sea about 50 million years ago in search of food. Here's how they became suited for swimming …

- their bodies became streamlined

- their front legs became flippers

- their back legs disappeared

- their nostrils became blow-holes on top of their heads

- their hair was replaced by blubber.

9 Instead of teeth, blue whales have huge, bony fringes hanging down the sides of their mouths. They use these like gigantic sieves for straining krill from the water.

10 And blue whales are BIG eaters. They eat tonnes of krill (see page 206) every day. So what would happen if you came face to face with one? Well, the answer is, nothing. Blue whales may be huge, but they're not interested in you … not when there's lip-smacking krill to gorge on!

Whopping whale sharks

So, if the blue whale isn't dangerous, what is? The biggest fish in the sea, perhaps? Wrong! The whopping great whale shark may be 18 metres long, measure several metres around its middle and weigh about 20 tonnes (that's four largish elephants). It also has the thickest skin of any living creature, as tough and leathery as rubber. And it has absolutely no sense of danger. Which is why it bashes into boats. But deadly? No. Colliding with boats is about as dangerous as the whale shark gets. In fact, this huge fish is completely harmless, and so easygoing that it will even let divers ride on its back. With skin that thick, it can't feel a thing anyway!

I WANT TO GET OFF AT THE NEXT STOP

A short, shark, shock!

OK, so whales and whale sharks won't get you, but there's bound to be something that will?

Picture the scene. One minute you're splashing about in the sea, minding your own business, and the next … you're on the menu for a hungry shark's lunch. A bit of an exaggeration? Or is it? Just how blood-curdling are these creatures? Is it really safe to go back into the water?

A shark's most fearsome features are its teeth. The gruesome great white has hundreds of spine-chilling choppers, as long as steak knives and razor sharp. This deadly hunter could easily bite you clean in two… Even dead, a shark can bite back. In 1977, an Australian fisherman was involved in a car crash. He was thrown on to the teeth of a dead shark's jaws, which happened to be lying on the back seat, and needed 22 stitches in his wounds! Ouch!

WANTED!

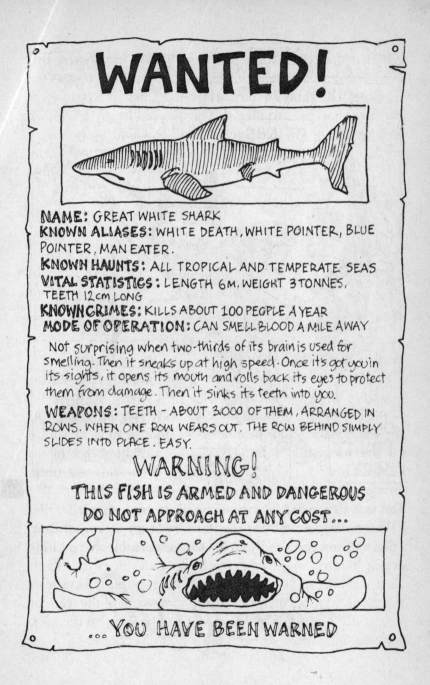

NAME: GREAT WHITE SHARK
KNOWN ALIASES: WHITE DEATH, WHITE POINTER, BLUE POINTER, MAN EATER.
KNOWN HAUNTS: ALL TROPICAL AND TEMPERATE SEAS
VITAL STATISTICS: LENGTH 6M, WEIGHT 3 TONNES, TEETH 12CM LONG
KNOWN CRIMES: KILLS ABOUT 100 PEOPLE A YEAR
MODE OF OPERATION: CAN SMELL BLOOD A MILE AWAY

Not surprising when two-thirds of its brain is used for smelling. Then it sneaks up at high speed. Once it's got you in its sights, it opens its mouth and rolls back its eyes to protect them from damage. Then it sinks its teeth into you.

WEAPONS: TEETH - ABOUT 3,000 OF THEM, ARRANGED IN ROWS. WHEN ONE ROW WEARS OUT, THE ROW BEHIND SIMPLY SLIDES INTO PLACE. EASY.

WARNING!
THIS FISH IS ARMED AND DANGEROUS
DO NOT APPROACH AT ANY COST...

... YOU HAVE BEEN WARNED

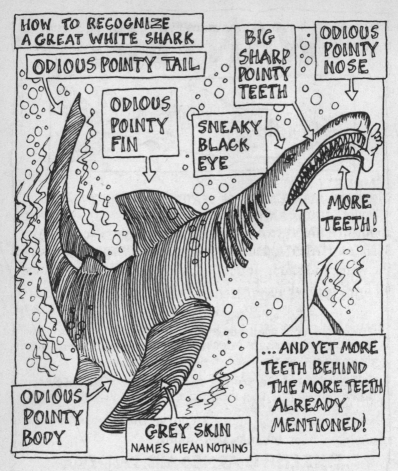

HOW TO RECOGNIZE A GREAT WHITE SHARK

ODIOUS POINTY TAIL

ODIOUS POINTY FIN

SNEAKY BLACK EYE

BIG SHARP POINTY TEETH

ODIOUS POINTY NOSE

MORE TEETH!

...AND YET MORE TEETH BEHIND THE MORE TEETH ALREADY MENTIONED!

ODIOUS POINTY BODY

GREY SKIN
NAMES MEAN NOTHING

Ten ways to avoid being snapped up by a shark
1 Wear a stripy swimming costume. With any luck, the shark will think you're a deadly stripy sea snake and leave you well alone.

2 Wear a stainless steel swimming suit, specially designed for the job. It's called a neptunic. It's made of thousands of metal rings. You might have some bruises but you won't get bitten.

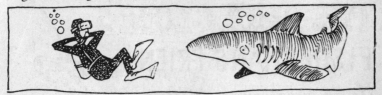

3 If you've even the tiniest cut or graze, don't go swimming. Sharks have a very sharp nose for blood…

4 Swim strongly with good, regular strokes. If you splash about weedily, a shark will think you're injured and eat you.

5 Try to startle the shark into submission. Slap the surface of the water and shout. It may not work but it'll keep you busy.

6 Don't swim alone. Sharks don't like company.

7 If you've got a shark after you, try to turn sharply and shake it off. They aren't as nimble as they look.

8 Don't swim at night, dawn or dusk. This is when most sharks are out and about.

9 If you're in a boat, try not to be seasick. The smell (and taste) of sick is irresistible to sharks.

10 And finally, great news for girls. Sharks are 13 times more likely to attack men than women!

But it's not just big creatures you need to beware of. Many smaller ones can hide a nasty surprise up their tentacles…

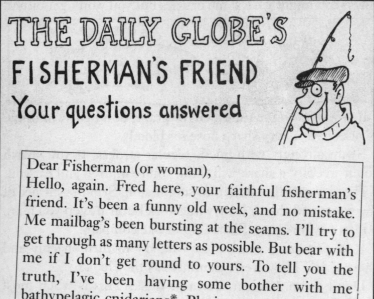

THE DAILY GLOBE'S
FISHERMAN'S FRIEND
Your questions answered

Dear Fisherman (or woman),
Hello, again. Fred here, your faithful fisherman's friend. It's been a funny old week, and no mistake. Me mailbag's been bursting at the seams. I'll try to get through as many letters as possible. But bear with me if I don't get round to yours. To tell you the truth, I've been having some bother with me bathypelagic cnidarians*. Playing me up something rotten they are. Right, then, here goes…

Dear Fred,
Someone gave me a cone shell for christmas and it's proving a real pain to train
What can I do?

Fred replies: Blimey, you've got a job on your hands. You see, training's the least of your problems. These little beauties don't like being messed about with

(*Roughly translated: Sea animals such as sea anemones and jellyfish that live at depths of between 1,000–4,000 metres down.)

288

Watch yourself, if you pick one up. You'll get a lethal dose of poison from a harpoon-like tooth, just under its shell. You won't have time to teach it to sit or stay. Within minutes, you won't be able to walk, speak or even breathe. A few hours later, you'll be dead, I'm afraid. I should take it back to the shop.

Dear Fred.
My Little brother says that if i keep nicking his trainers, he'll put octopus spit in my tea. should i be scared? (Ps please don't tell my parents i wrote in, im meant to be doing my geography homework.)

Fred replies: You young people, I don't know. Wasn't like that in my day. Still, I don't suppose it will hurt just this once. Where was I? Oh, yes, well, it all depends on what sort of octopus your brother uses. If it's a blue-ringed octopus, you're in trouble. This little creature kills more people a year than man-eating sharks. Its spit, in particular, is horribly poisonous. If I were you, I'd save up me pocket money and buy me own pair of trainers instead.

★ STAR LETTER ★

The writer of this week's star letter wins a day out with Fred on his sturdy old boat, *The Selfish Shellfish*. (If you get seasick, you'll have to make do with a signed photo instead.)

DEAR FRED,
IF A PERSON (NOT ME) WANTED TO MURDER SOMEONE (WHICH OF COURSE, THEY DON'T), IS THERE ANYTHING IN THE SEA THEY COULD USE?

Fred replies: Now, let me think. Bit of a fishy sort of question, this one. You could use Portuguese man-of-war tentacles. They're good and poisonous, I happen to know. I read somewhere, I forget where it was now, that they were once used in a murder attempt. Made into a soup, I believe they were. But the victim had a strong stomach and pulled through. Feeding someone to a shark would probably be quicker, if you ask me.

Dear Fred,
I can't tell me stones from me fish, can you help?

Fred replies: I know how you feel. It's a tricky one, this. Normally, stones look like stones and fish look like fish. But there is one very nasty exception. A stonefish looks like a stone and acts like a stone, until you tread on it... *Then* it spears you with its poisonous spines, perishin' thing. You'll be ranting and raving, you won't be able to help yourself. Then you'll be in pain like you've never felt before, and then you'll drop dead. If you're lucky. I should steer well clear, if I was you.

Dear Fred,
Yesterday I trod on a stingray. My leg's gone all blue and lumpy. Will it fall off?

Fred replies: It might, you know. I should get yourself off to the doctor. You see, the spike at the end of a stingray's tail is loaded with poison. What on Earth were you doing to get it so upset? You must have pestered it rotten for it to lash out like that. Stingrays like a quiet life, usually. By the way, if you've still got the spike, you could always turn it into a letter opener. People do, I'm told.

Dear Fred,
The lads and I have been having a bet on which is the deadliest creature in the sea? We just can't seem to agree. I say the tuna fish but the others just laugh. Can you settle things once and for all?

Fred replies: The tuna fish? Don't talk daft. But mind you, it could turn nasty if you were a small, tasty fish. Then you'd be lovely for lunch. But the most dangerous sea creature is the sea wasp jellyfish. It's small but deadly, and could kill you in a few minutes flat. Its tentacles ooze poison (enough in one jellyfish to kill 60 people). And it's so sneaky and see-through, you might not even notice it until it's too late. And that's not just my opinion. Ask anyone.

You could, for example, ask two scientists whose life's work was to study these odious creatures. And not always from a safe distance.

Killers down under
A pier off the coast of Australia, summer 1977
The scientists peered into the dark water along the edge of the pier. At last, they had found what they were looking for. There, bobbing and shimmering in the glare of the floodlights, were two ghostly shapes, with strings of ghastly tentacles streaming out behind their boxlike bodies. They

were face to face with the infamous *Chironex fleckeri* (Latin for 'old bendy hand'). That's a sea wasp to you. The most venomous creature in the sea. This was the moment they had been waiting for.

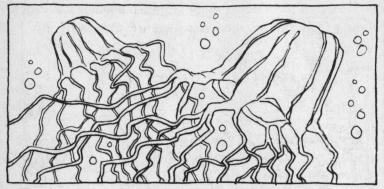

But how were they going to catch the killer jellyfish? If you're stung by a sea wasp, you can kiss goodbye to any thoughts of Christmas presents. You may not be there to open them. First, there's the unbearable pain, followed by problems breathing. Your heart stops pumping. In four minutes or less, unless you get treatment, you're dead. So, why on Earth try to catch this dastardly duo? Why not leave well alone, and go and study something else less sinister?

No. These were scientists on a mission – to capture a fully-grown sea wasp (which has a body the size of a basketball, only square, and 60-odd tentacles five metres long. Armed with masses of deadly stings). Besides, the scientists had a cunning plan. First, they had to cover up. They put on long trousers, long-sleeved shirts and gloves, taped tightly at the wrists. Then they grabbed some large plastic buckets and long-handled nets and set off for the pier. At first, everything went according to plan. Using the nets to push and shove, they coaxed the sea wasps into the buckets and hoisted them out of the water. So far, so good. Then disaster struck.

Catching the jellyfish was proving hot work and one of the scientists took his shirt off. BIG mistake. As he hauled a bucket out of the water, a single sea wasp tentacle was caught in the breeze and brushed ever so gently against his arm.

It was only the slightest, most glancing of touches – but the scientist felt as if his skin was on fire. An ugly, raw, red stripe snaked down his arm. And the pain! The pain was worse than anything he had ever known. But he was lucky. He had only been struck by a couple of centimetres of tentacle. It takes about three metres to be fatal. He didn't even want to think about that. And he didn't want to think about giving in either. Luckily, he pulled through.

Back at the lab the scientists took a close look at the sea wasp. No one had ever been this close. By looking at their beastly bodies, the scientists were going to be the first to find out how jellyfish live and breed – and, most importantly, examine their deadly poison. Information that could help to save lives.

DON'T PANIC! There are various things you can do if you're stung by a sea wasp. Which one would you think works best?

A DAB WITH VINEGAR

B DRINK ANTIVENOM

C WEAR TWO PAIRS OF TIGHTS

Answer: b) Your best option. But you need to act quickly and get to hospital fast. Antivenom is a medicine which stops venom (poison) working. It's injected into your muscles or veins and works almost immediately. By the way, a) can help in an emergency but you need to follow up with b). And c) isn't as silly as it sounds. Surfers entering sea wasp-infested waters sometimes wear two pairs of tights – one on their legs and one on their arms and heads – to protect them from jellyfish stings.

Dark doings deep down

OK, so most sea creatures aren't anything like as dangerous as sea wasps, but the places they live in can be deadly. For fish who live in the darkest depths of the sea, life can really get you down.

Not only is it…

Horribly cold – in the depths of the odious oceans, the water is f-f-freezing cold.

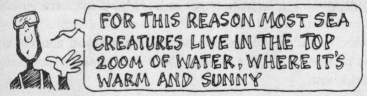

FOR THIS REASON MOST SEA CREATURES LIVE IN THE TOP 200M OF WATER, WHERE IT'S WARM AND SUNNY

...and pitch black – when sunlight hits the sea, some bounces back into the sky and some is absorbed by the water. But it only reaches a short way down. Below about 250 metres, the water is black as night.

It's also...

Deeply depressing – the deeper you go underwater, the greater the weight of the water pressing down on you. For each ten metres you descend, the pressure increases by one kilogram per one square centimetre. It's crushing.

...and lonely – friendly faces are few and far between when you're a kilometre or more beneath the waves.

And it really is...

Very dangerous – there's not much food about down there so you have to watch your back. Deep-sea creatures eat worms, crustaceans and anything else they can get their teeth into. They also rely on the dead bodies of plants and animals raining down from above. These can take some time to reach them...

Despite all this, there are some odious ocean dwellers for whom these dangerous depths are home, sweet home. But how on Earth do they survive? Meet the distracting deep-sea angler fish...

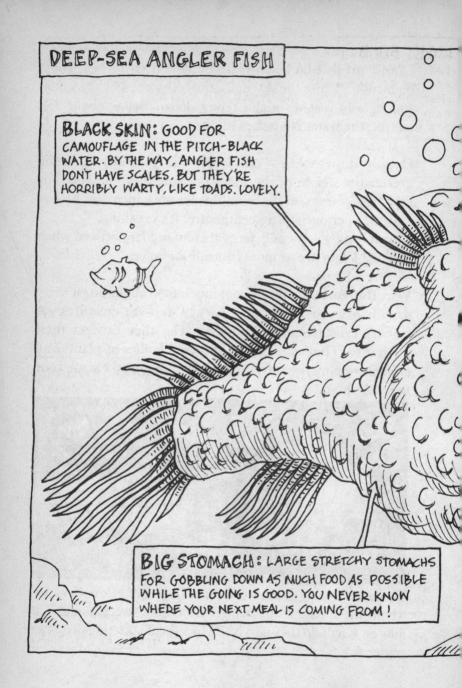

DEEP-SEA ANGLER FISH

BLACK SKIN: GOOD FOR CAMOUFLAGE IN THE PITCH-BLACK WATER. BY THE WAY, ANGLER FISH DON'T HAVE SCALES, BUT THEY'RE HORRIBLY WARTY, LIKE TOADS. LOVELY.

BIG STOMACH: LARGE STRETCHY STOMACHS FOR GOBBLING DOWN AS MUCH FOOD AS POSSIBLE WHILE THE GOING IS GOOD. YOU NEVER KNOW WHERE YOUR NEXT MEAL IS COMING FROM!

LIGHT BULB: YES, LIGHT BULB. HOW ELSE WOULD YOU SEE IN THE DARK? THE LIGHT BULB DANGLES OVER THE FISH'S MOUTH ON A LONG FIN LIKE A FISHING ROD. IT'S A BLOB, MADE UP OF MILLIONS OF TINY LIGHT-GIVING BACTERIA. THE ANGLER FISH ALSO USES ITS LIGHT AS BAIT. SMALL FISH MISTAKE IT FOR A SNACK AND SWIM TOWARDS IT. STRAIGHT INTO THE ANGLER'S MOUTH.

BIG MOUTH: HUGE AND LINED WITH NASTY LONG GNASHERS WHICH CURVE BACKWARDS. WHY? WELL THEY LET PREY IN, NICE AS PIE, THEN THEY SPRING FORWARD AND SLAM SHUT! LIKE A ROW OF PRISON BARS, SO THE PREY CAN'T GET OUT!

LUMPY BODY: ANGLER FISH DON'T HAVE SLEEK, STREAMLINED BODIES, LIKE OTHER FISH, BECAUSE THEY DON'T NEED TO SWIM FAST TO CATCH THEIR FOOD. IN FACT, THEY'RE REALLY RATHER FLABBY AND SLOW. SOME SPEND ALL DAY LYING AROUND ON THE SEABED, MOUTHS WIDE OPEN, WAITING FOR FOOD TO SWIM IN!

BUT ANGLER FISH AREN'T THE ONLY FISH TO SEE IN THE DARK

How on Earth do they do it?

1 Over half of all deep-sea fish make their own light. Some glow because of chemical reactions inside their bodies. Others use clumps of bacteria as torches.

2 What do you think sea creatures use their lights for? To...

A FIND FOOD...

B FIND MATES...

C FIND THEIR WAY IN THE DARK...

D SCARE OFF ATTACKERS... BEAT IT!

E TALK TO EACH OTHER... DOT DOT DASH   DOT DASH DOT

Answer: All of these are true.

3 Flashlight fish have a light under each eye. They can turn them on and off by covering them up with shutters of skin, like tiny curtains. A handy trick for puzzling predators. The

flashlights are bright enough to light up a small room. And they carry on glowing even after the fish has snuffed it.

4 Twinkle, twinkle, little seastar! Some seastars (they're related to starfish) glow green and blue as a warning to predators that they taste terrible.

5 Little firefly squid use their lights for camouflage and to get to know a mate. They also squirt enemies with luminous blue goo which gives them time to make a quick getaway. In Japan, fishermen bait their lines with slithers of these sparkling squid.

Earth-shattering fact
During the Second World War, Japanese sailors hit upon a way of saving electricity. They rubbed their hands with some luminous bacteria found inside shellfish. This gave just enough light to read top-secret files by, but not enough to alert enemy warships.

Armed and dangerous

In the depths of the ocean, it's a fish–eat–fish world. If you can't fight back, you'll soon go under. Many sea creatures are well-equipped for survival, with stings, sharp teeth, prickles and poison. Some are more cunning than others. Here are a few of the tricks they have tucked up their fins…

Sharp-shooter The no–nonsense pistol shrimp shoots its food down at close range. It simply takes aim … and fires, snapping its right claw with a noise like gunshot. This sends shock waves racing through the water, stunning the victim while the shrimp moves in for the kill.

Getting the point Needlefish are long, thin, and extremely painful when pestered. A sailor in the USA was once pinned to his boat when a needled needlefish leapt out of the sea and stuck straight through his leg.

Second-hand poison Sea slugs don't have weapons of their own to protect them from being eaten. So they gobble down sea anemones, complete with stings, and use them instead. The anemones' stings pass through the sea slug's body and lie just under its skin. If a famished fish brushes past, the stings stick into it. Ouch!

A shocking tail The black torpedo ray stuns prey and predators by shocking them with electricity (made in its head). A fisherman in England once caught a torpedo ray and put it on display. He charged spectators a small fee to guess its weight. It made his fortune. No one could hold on to the ray for long enough to get a proper feel!

Armless fun

When a starfish wants to distract an attacker, it simply leaves an arm or two behind. Weird or what? Try this quick quiz to see what you know about the very strange starfish:

1 Starfish can have up to 40 arms. TRUE/FALSE?

2 Starfish don't have heads. TRUE/FALSE?

3 The biggest starfish ever found was the size of a dustbin lid. TRUE/FALSE?

4 Starfish spend their day mugging molluscs. TRUE/FALSE?

5 Starfish have terrible table manners. TRUE/FALSE?

Answers:
1 True. If a starfish loses an arm (see above), it just grows another one. What's more, it can grow a whole new body from a tiny piece of arm (though it takes a year or two). And mistakes can happen. Some starfish end up with four or 40 arms, instead of the usual five or six.

301

2 True. But they do have eyes on the ends of their arms. Because they don't have a head, they don't have a brain either! A starfish's body is basically just a mouth and stomach on legs (or arms).

3 False. The biggest starfish are actually twice as big as a dustbin lid! They measure almost 1.5 metres across the tips of their arms. Yet their bodies are only 2.5 centimetres wide. The smallest starfish are a paltry 5 millimetres across. You could easily fit one on your thumbnail.

4 True. Under each arm, a starfish has a row of tiny suckers (called tube feet). When a starfish fancies a snack, it wraps its arms tightly around a mollusc so that it's stuck fast, prises it open, then gobbles it up.

5 True. The crown-of-thorns starfish is particularly bad. When it wants to crunch on a piece of coral, it sicks out its stomach over the coral, digests it slowly outside its body, then pulls its stomach in again. Disgusting! And if that's not bad enough, the crown-of-thorns is also the only poisonous starfish, packing a punch with its needle-sharp spines. They are currently eating their way through the Great Barrier Reef!

You can't blame a starfish for trying. The truth is, that, lovely or loathsome, prickly or poisonous, every single sea creature has something to fear. Even the big ones. But the greatest risk isn't from each other. It's much, much worse than that. There's one creature all fish should be scared of. Guess who?

SEA SICK

For centuries, humans have been using the oceans as a gigantic dustbin. It's true! The oceans are so huge, that tipping any old rubbish into the sea seemed quite a good way to lose it for ever. But every year, 26 billion tonnes of rubbish, sewage, old industrial chemicals, oil and even radioactive waste finds its way into the salty sea. And it's all still there, somewhere. No wonder it's making the sea sick. All this pollution has a fatal effect on sea animals and plants, too. It even has harmful effects on humans. And it's taking its toll on some of the most beautiful features of the sea.

Coral reefs at risk

If it's life and colour you're after, visit a coral reef. The busiest places in the big, blue sea. The biggest can grow as large as islands, yet they're built by creatures no larger than ants. And they're dying. Over 10 per cent of reefs have gone already and another 60 per cent are seriously sick. But why on Earth do coral reefs matter? Try this quiz to find out more. Better still, try it out on someone else, your mum, dad, teacher…

Coral conundrum

1 What on Earth is coral made from?
a) rocks
b) animals
c) plants

2 How many of these creatures are at home on a coral reef?
a) lionfish
b) giant clams
c) moray eels
d) clownfish
e) butterfly fish
f) feather stars
g) reef sharks
h) parrot fish
i) sea snakes
j) nudibranchs

3 Where on Earth do parrot fish sleep?
a) on the seabed
b) on a coral ledge
c) in a sleeping-bag

4 How fast does a coral reef grow?
a) about 5 millimetres a year
b) about 2.5 centimetres a year
c) about 1 kilometre a year

5 Where on Earth are most coral reefs found?
a) in the Pacific Ocean
b) in the Atlantic Ocean
c) in the Indian Ocean

6 The Great Barrier Reef off north-east Australia is so huge, you can see it from…?
a) the moon
b) New Zealand
c) south-west Australia

7 Which of these can be made from coral?
a) teeth
b) eyes
c) bones

8 What on Earth is a coral atoll?
a) a coral island
b) a coral fish
c) a piece of coral shaped like a brain

9 Coral reefs are in danger from…?
a) souvenir collectors
b) oil exploration
c) pollution
d) fishing boats
e) cutting down trees on land

10 What on Earth can we do to save them?
a) dig them up and move them elsewhere
b) turn them into marine parks
c) build glass tanks around them

Answers:

1b) Scientists used to think coral was made from plants. In fact, coral reefs are built by tiny animals, called polyps. They're close relatives of the jellyfish and of sea anemones. They live together in groups of millions and millions. Coral is actually the hard, stony cases which the polyps build to protect their soft, squashy bodies, using chemicals from the water. Most of a reef is made of empty white cases (the polyps inside having long since died). But the colourful top layer is very much alive.

2 The answer is all of them. Coral reefs are teeming with life. In fact, they're home to so much sea life that they're known as the gardens of the sea. A third of all types of fish live among them with thousands of other cool creatures for company. Never heard of a nudibranch? It's a fancy name for a brightly-coloured sea slug. The colours are a warning: "Go away and leave me alone. I taste horrible!"

3c) The parrot fish has very strange sleeping habits. At night, it blows a sticky bubble of jelly around its body, like a sleeping-bag, then dozes off inside. Safe and snug from its enemies, like moray eels. They can't smell the parrot fish while it's in its bed.

4b) Coral grows at the same speed as your fingernails, about 2.5 centimetres a year. At this rate, a reef takes millions of years to grow. Scientists can date reefs by giving them X-rays, just like the ones doctors use to look at your insides. These show tiny rings on the polyps' coral cases. Each ring takes a year to grow. The Great Barrier Reef in Australia is at least 18 million years old.

5c) Over half of all coral reefs are in the Indian Ocean where conditions are perfect for the corals to grow. (There are also reefs in the Pacific and Atlantic.) Corals like warm, sunny and shallow waters best. If the sea level rises, or gets too cold, the coral gets sick and dies. Sunlight is vital. The polyps grow in partnership with tiny plants (algae) which help to glue the reef together. And algae need sunlight to make their food. If the water is dirty, this can also stunt the corals' growth.

6a) The Great Barrier Reef is over 2,000 kilometres long and covers over 200,000 sqare kilometres (that's twice the size of Iceland). It's the biggest coral reef in the world and the biggest structure made by any living things, including us. Wow!

7b) and **c)** Believe it or not, coral eye sockets and bones are already being fitted in humans. Coral is perfect for the job because its structure (it's full of tiny holes) is similar to real human bone. At present, though, only three of the 2,500 types of coral can be used to make body bits. These are found in the South Pacific where islanders already use coral to build everything from houses and jewellery to sewer pipes! Only a very small amount of coral – about enough to fill the boot of a car – is harvested each year for surgery. And it's removed very carefully so the reef isn't ruined.

8a) Coral atolls begin life as reefs growing on the slopes of volcanoes. Over the years, the volcanoes sink into the sea. But the coral keeps growing to form a horseshoe-shaped island around a sleepy lagoon. The Pacific Ocean is full of them. Heavenly for holidays!

9 Sadly, the answer is all of these. Tonnes and tonnes of coral are stolen for jewellery, ornaments and for decorating people's aquariums. Reefs are blasted with explosives in the search for oil. They're also poisoned by pollution and smothered by soil which slops into the sea when trees are cut down on land. Fishing is a tricky problem. Millions of people rely on reef fish for their food. But fishing boats can smash up the coral as they dredge the reef for fish and shellfish.

10b) The good news is that, left well alone, coral reefs can recover. Some countries have turned their reefs into parks which are guarded day and night. Tourists and divers have to pay to visit and woe betide anyone caught taking bits home.

Horrible human habits

But we humans are still pretty horrible. If we want to make the sea really sick, we're going the right way about it. Here are just some of our sick habits…

1 Pump it

What we do: Pump stinking sewage straight into the sea. And let chemicals and pesticides from farms keep washing into the sea from our rivers.

What's so sick about that? Plankton (tiny plants) eat up the sewage and other chemicals, then it grows and grows. And grows. Until it covers the sea in thick, green slime. The sinister slime blocks out sunlight which other plants need to make food. And when it dies, it's eaten by bacteria which starve the water of oxygen, so fish and shellfish suffocate.

Why we won't stop: More than half the world's people live close to the coast, so it's the simplest way to wash away our waste and wash our hands of the problem.

2 Leak it

What we do: Leak poisonous metals, such as mercury and lead, into the sea from factories, mines and boats.

What's so sick about that? The metals are digested by fish, then move up the food chain until they reach people, with fatal effects. In the 1950s, hundreds of people in Japan suffered brain damage after eating fish that was poisoned with mercury. It had leaked into the sea from a nearby chemical factory.

Why we won't stop: Factories supply us with many of the things we use in our daily lives, from cars and food to nuts and bolts. And mines produce raw materials. People are now experimenting with cleaner ways of going about things but it's a long, slow process.

3 Dump it

What we do: Dump radioactive waste from nuclear power stations on land into the sea in a concrete case.

What's so sick about that? This waste is deadly poisonous. Even in its concrete case, it can take thousands of years to become safe. If it leaks into the water, it could cause cancer and other fatal diseases (in humans and sea animals).

Why we won't stop: Because we don't really know what else to do with it. Imagine the outcry if it was buried on land. Out of sight is out of mind.

4 Chuck it

What we do: Dump millions of tonnes of rubbish – plastic bags, bottles, oil drums, barrels, tins and ropes – into the sea every year. Five million tonnes of this is chucked over the sides of ships.

What's so sick about that? Thousands of sea birds, mammals, turtles and fish get caught up in old ropes and nets, and die as they try to escape. And piles of rubbish are washed up on beaches when the tide comes in. Now that's pretty sick!

Why we won't stop: We make so much rubbish that it can't all be disposed of on land. Already, billions of tonnes is buried underground. This is OK for rubbish that rots away, but plastics and metals last for ages. Basically, we need to throw away less rubbish, or recycle materials like plastic and glass. As for all those old ropes and nets, fishermen need to tidy up after themselves. Or else.

5 Spill it

What we do: Run oil-tankers aground and spill millions of litres of oil into the sea.

What's so sick about that? The oil clogs birds' feathers so they can't keep warm or stay afloat, and they die. Other sea creatures are poisoned when they try to swallow the oil. Some of the chemicals used to soak up the oil are even more dangerous. It can take years and years to clean up the mess.

Why we won't stop: Oil makes the world go round. It fuels our cars, factories, homes, you name it. But it's also a killer. Oil companies need to be more responsible – and, to be fair, many are trying. For example, some oil tankers are now made with double thickness walls to help prevent any leaks. But it all costs a great deal of money. Basically, we want cheap petrol so tankers are run cheaply.

6 Drill it

What we do: Pollute the sea with noise from ships, by drilling into the seabed and testing out new weapons under water.

What's so sick about that? Sound waves carry well underwater and many sea creatures have sensitive hearing. Imagine living in *that* din.

Why we won't stop: We don't have to hear it, so we turn a deaf ear. Of course, it would be different if you were just about to drop off to sleep at night when someone started drilling into the pavement outside your window, wouldn't it?

Earth-shattering fact
The North Sea is now so disgustingly dirty that, in ten years'
time, fish like mackerel, cod and haddock could be extinct.
So enjoy those fish and chips ... while you still can.

No wonder the sea's sick. Wouldn't you be?

Do we need the oceans more than they need us?

You can make up your own mind by reading about three of the things we wouldn't have without the odious oceans.

Rotten rain The oceans play a vital part in the weather. Here's what happens:

1 The sun warms up the oceans and millions of litres of water rises into the sky as (invisible) water vapour.

2 As the vapour rises, it cools and turns back into liquid water.

3 Then it falls as rain.

4 On land, rivers carry the water back into the sea.

5 Then the whole thing starts all over again.

You might think less rain would be a good thing. Then geography field trips wouldn't be so wet and soggy. Think again. Without the rain, no plants could grow, and without plants, there'd be no food. Oceans are also crucial for controlling the Earth's temperature, by absorbing and releasing heaps of heat and sharing it out more evenly.

Amazing oxygen Without the oceans, you wouldn't be able to breathe. The sea is full of tiny green plants, called algae, which make over half of all the oxygen we breathe. How? Well, algae don't need to go shopping for food. They make their own. They use sunlight to turn carbon dioxide (a gas) and water into food. And oxygen.

Tuna fish sandwiches Millions of people on Earth rely on the oceans for food. Not just tasty tuna fish but crabby crustaceans, meaty molluscs, seaweed, salt and so on. The problem is that so many fish are caught that stocks are running dangerously low. Talking of tuna, in the last 20 years, stocks of tuna in the West Atlantic have dropped by a massive 90 per cent. The chips are down.

Saving the sea

The seas have certainly ended up in a pretty sick state, but things aren't quite as gloomy as they sound. Campaigns are helping to make us all aware of the terrible state of affairs. 1997 was the International Year of the Reef. You could help out by adopting your own chunk of coral reef – you can adopt a whale, too, if you think you can cope!

1998 was officially the International Year of the Ocean. Governments all round the world were asked to clean up their acts and try to cut down on polluting the water and hauling too many fish from the sea. These efforts include international conventions to prevent pollution by aircraft and ships. It was also agreed that the best way to persuade people to save the sea was by encouraging them to get to know it better. It's too early to say yet whether this idea has worked. But there's still plenty of time for you to pop down to your nearest beach and make friends with the not-so-odious oceans.

If you're still interested in finding out more, here
are some websites you can visit:

http://www.amrivers.org/
North America's leading national river conservation
organization

http://www.cis.umassd.edu/~gleung/
Yellow River, the longest river in China, has its own
homepage!

http://www.irn.org/
International Rivers Network, working to halt destructive
river development projects

http://www.highway57.co.uk/tbvc
Find out about the Thames Barrier, the world's largest
movable flood barrier.

http://www.nps:gov/yose/note3.htm
A waterfall picture book from Yosemite National Park,
California.

http://www.amazonthefilm.com/
The official Amazon river website with photos, a quiz and
even an Amazon movie!

http://www.whaletimes.org/
Find out how your favourite animals survive in the ocean
... and put your own questions to Jake the Seadog.

www.londonaquarium.co.uk
Dive through the oceans of the world and meet their
horrible inhabitants in this virtual marine museum.

www.wln.com/~deltapac.ocean_od.html
A great collection of places to go for an ocean odyssey,
without even getting your feet wet.

www.oceansconservation.com/education./ystudnts.htm
More salty sites and leviathan links.

www.greenpeace.org.uk/greenbytes/index.html
A special web page for budding "greens". Learn all about
Greenpeace and its campaign to save our seas.

www.discovery.com/area/science/titanic/titanicopener.html
Travel several kilometres under the ocean with explorers
and film crews to visit Titanic's watery grave.

www.royal-navy.mod.uk/index.htm
Fancy a life at sea? See if naval life would make you a sea
Captain, or just plain sea sick!

Horrible Geography

Geography with the gritty bits left in!

Have you seen:

Violent Volcanoes

Stormy Weather

Desperate Deserts

Earth-shattering Earthquakes

Freaky Peaks

Bloomin' Rainforests

Perishing Poles

Intrepid Explorers

Wild Islands